**Everyman's Poetry**

*Everyman, I will go with thee,*
*and be thy guide*

# Robert Burns

Selected and edited by DONALD A. LOW

University of Stirling

EVERYMAN
J. M. Dent · London

This edition first published by Everyman Paperbacks in 1996
Selection, introduction and other critical apparatus © J. M. Dent 1996

J. M. Dent
Orion Publishing Group
Orion House
5 Upper St Martin's Lane
London WC2H 9EA

Typeset by Deltatype Ltd, Ellesmere Port, Cheshire
Printed in Great Britain by
The Guernsey Press Co. Ltd, Guernsey, C.I.

British Library Cataloguing-in-Publication
Data is available upon request.

ISBN 0 460 87814 X

# Contents

# Note on the Author and Editor

ROBERT BURNS (1759–96) was the eldest son of an unsuccessful tenant farmer in Ayrshire. Growing up to a life of demanding physical work, poverty and awareness of social disadvantage, he began to write poetry in an attempt to find 'some kind of counterpoise' to these harsh realities. By his mid twenties, he was an accomplished poet and song-writer, especially in his native Scots. In the summer of 1786, when he was on the point of giving up farming in Scotland and emigrating to the West Indies essentially because of a broken love affair with a local girl, Burns published his first collection of poems, printed in the county town of Kilmarnock. *Poems, Chiefly In The Scottish Dialect* met with such acclaim in Ayrshire and among West of Scotland people in Edinburgh that he changed all his plans, and travelled to the capital, where he was welcomed by a number of leading literary figures.

Among those who saluted the new arrival was Henry Mackenzie, whose sentimental novel *The Man of Feeling* Burns intensely admired. Mackenzie praised the 'power of genius' of 'this Heaven-taught ploughman' in an influential essay in his periodical *The Lounger*, and helped Burns arrange publication of an expanded edition of his *Poems* in the spring of 1787.

When Burns received part of the money which the new edition earned for him, he made a number of tours, to the Borders and to the Highlands. Otherwise, apart from a return visit to Ayrshire, he was to spend the winter of 1787–8 in Edinburgh also. Later, he lived in Dumfriesshire and became an Excise Officer.

Burns's literary work in the remaining years of his life consists of many outstanding songs, and the poem 'Tam o' Shanter'.

DONALD A. LOW is Professor of English Studies at the University of Stirling. His publications on Burns include *Poems In Scots And English* (Everyman Paperbacks, 1993) and *The Songs of Robert Burns* (Routledge, 1993). He studied at St Andrews and Pembroke College, Cambridge.

# Chronology of Burns's Life

| Year | Life |
| --- | --- |
| 1759 | Born at Alloway, near Ayr, 25 January, first child of Agnes and William Burns, tenant farmer |
| 1765 | Taught, with his brother Gilbert, by John Murdoch, hired as their instructor by William Burns and a group of neighbours |
| 1766 | Father begins to farm Mount Oliphant, a 70-acre farm near Alloway |
| 1768 | Father continues his sons' education himself when Murdoch leaves for a teaching appointment in Dumfries. Agnes Burns shares with Robert many songs and stories, which include legends of the supernatural |
| 1772 | Robert and Gilbert go to school week about in Dalrymple, four miles from Ayr |
| 1773 | Murdoch returns to teach English in Ayr. Burns studies French, English Grammar, Latin |
| 1774 | Writes his first song at harvest-time to impress a pretty girl called Nelly |

# Chronology of his Times

| Year | Artistic Context | Historical Events |
|------|------------------|-------------------|
| 1759 | Voltaire, *Candide* Haydn, First Symphony Johnson, 'Rasselas' | British Museum opens |
| 1760 | Macpherson, *Fragments of Ancient Poetry, Collected in The Highlands of Scotland* | Death of George II; succeeded by George III, his grandson |
| 1764 | Walpole, *The Castle of Otranto* | |
| 1765 | Percy, *Reliques of Ancient English Poetry* | |
| 1766 | Goldsmith, *The Vicar of Wakefield* | |
| 1769 | | Birth of Napoleon Bonaparte |
| 1769–70 | | James Cook's first voyage round the world; east coast of Australia discovered |
| 1770 | Goldsmith, 'The Deserted Village' | First public restaurant opens in Paris |
| 1773 | | Boston Tea Party: American protest against tea duty |
| 1774 | Goethe, *Sorrows of Werther* | First Congress of the 13 Colonies, except Georgia, meets at Philadelphia; Quebec Act establishes rights of French Canadians |

| Year | Life |
|------|------|
| 1777 | Family move to Lochlie, a 130-acre farm near the village of Tarbolton, where Burns attends a dancing class 'to give my manners a brush' |
| 1780 | With six friends forms The Tarbolton Bachelors' Club, a debating society which meets once a month |
| 1781 | Goes to Irvine to learn flax-making. He is inducted as a mason into St David's Lodge, no. 174, Tarbolton |
| 1782 | Returns to Lochlie when the flax shop is burned to the ground owing to 'the drunken carelessness of my Partner's wife' |
| 1783 | Begins his first Commonplace Book. He and Gilbert secretly arrange to lease Mossgiel, a farm of 118 acres, near the village of Mauchline, to help the family's economic circumstances and their dying father |
| 1784 | Death of William Burns in February. The next month the family move into Mossgiel |
| 1785 | Meets Jean Armour at a Mauchline dance. He begins to 'puzzle Calvinism with heat and indiscretion' and writes much poetry. 22 May, birth of Elizabeth, his daughter by Elizabeth Paton |
| 1786 | Relationships under much stress. April, proposals for *Poems, Chiefly In The Scottish Dialect* published; book itself is published at Kilmarnock on 31 July in an edition of 600 copies at a price of 3s. |
| 1787 | April, first Edinburgh edition of *Poems*. When he receives part of the money which the new edition earns for him, he makes a number of tours, to the Borders and repeatedly to the Highlands. Begins to contribute songs to James Johnson's *Scots Musical Museum* (1787–1803), virtually as the song collection's literary editor. Meets Mrs Agnes McLehose ('Clarinda'). 20 October, first London edition of *Poems* |
| 1787–8 | Much of this winter spent in Edinburgh |

| Year | Artistic Context | Historical Events |
|------|------------------|-------------------|
| 1776 | Smith, *Inquiry Into the Nature and Causes of the Wealth of Nations* | American Declaration of Independence |
| 1778 | Sheridan, *The School for Scandal* | |
| 1781 | Rousseau, *Confessions* Kant, *Critique of Pure Reason* | |
| 1783 | | England recognizes USA; First aerial voyages, by hot-air and hydrogen balloons, invented by the Montgolfier brothers and S. A. C. Charles |
| 1784 | | Vincent Lunardi, first balloon flight over England |
| 1787 | Mozart, *Don Giovanni* | |

| Year | Life |
|------|------|
| 1788 | Accepts Jean Armour as his wife ('and so farewell Rakery!'), leases the farm of Ellisland, near Dumfries, and is commissioned as an Exciseman. From now on, writes more songs than poems |
| 1789 | Begins work in the Excise at a salary of £50 per annum |
| 1790 | Writes 'Tam o' Shanter' |
| 1791 | Gives up Ellisland in favour of full-time Excise work and moves to Dumfries. On a visit to Edinburgh, says farewell to Clarinda |
| 1792 | Asked to contribute songs to George Thomson's *A Select Collection of Scottish Airs* (1793–1818) |
| 1793 | Second Edinburgh edition of *Poems* and first set of Thomson's *Select Collection* |
| 1794 | Appointed Acting Supervisor of Excise |
| 1795 | Joins in organizing Dumfries Volunteers. Severely ill with rheumatic fever |
| 1796 | 21 July, dies at Dumfries |

| Year | Artistic Context | Historical Events |
| --- | --- | --- |
| 1788 | | Death of Charles Edward Stuart ('Bonnie Prince Charlie') |
| 1789 | Blake, *Songs of Innocence* | Fall of the Bastille: French Revolution; George Washington becomes President of USA |
| 1790 | Paine, *The Rights of Man* Burke, *Reflections on the French Revolution* | |
| 1791 | Boswell, *The Life of Samuel Johnson, LL.D.* | First ten amendments to USA Constitution; Washington, DC founded |
| 1792 | | French Republic established |
| 1793 | | First Coalition against France; France declares war on Britain |
| 1794 | Blake, *Songs of Experience* | Beginning of friendship between Goethe and Schiller |
| 1795 | | Speenhamland Act (Poor Law) wages supplemented by doles |
| 1798 | Wordsworth and Coleridge, *Lyrical Ballads* | |

# Introduction

What kind of poet is Burns and what is special about him? It would no doubt be possible to repeat claims made in the past about 'Scotland's National Bard' but, in the final years of the twentieth century, it is time to focus on the essential qualities of Robert Burns the writer which endure and to set aside dated notions from two hundred years ago which are now merely history.

Biographical issues have their own interest, but are secondary to his literary art. Yes, Burns had a reputation as a lover of women and as someone who liked whisky; but above all he was an exceptionally gifted poet and songwriter, one who shares with the reader honesty and humour as primary values. Scandal and sexual notoriety were present in Burns's life, but it is his poetic art which lives on and gives his work its power. In a sense, Burns resembles the great twentieth-century painter Pablo Picasso. Neither was free from human error, but despite weaknesses the creative work of each deserves to survive. Each celebrated natural creation and enjoyed experimentation – Burns in verse form and song, Picasso in collage, ceramics and sculpture as well as painting. Irony exists in Burns's love of the fiddle and in Picasso's early paintings of the guitar. Picasso commented in 1949:

> We artists are indestructible; even in a prison, or in a concentration camp, I would be almighty in my own world of art, even if I had to paint my pictures with my wet tongue on the dusty floor of my cell.

For Burns likewise, the creation of a day's poem or song mattered like breath. Life was hard as a tenant farmer and while the writing of poetry might not succeed in bringing about a change in his personal circumstances, it was a congenial form of activity in its own right and one which gave him an outlet for his ideas to set against the drudgery of working on the land. Burns the writer is versatile, and his poetry shows that he chooses to vary his style according to the context. It is clear that, above all, Burns rhymed for his own pleasure and for fun. He explains in his epistle 'To J. S****':

> Some rhyme a neebor's name to lash;
> Some rhyme, (vain thought!) for needfu' cash;
> Some rhyme to court the countra clash,
>     An' raise a din;
> For me, an *aim* I never fash;
>     I rhyme for *fun*.

More formally than in the verses to James Smith, in his Preface to *Poems, Chiefly In The Scottish Dialect* published at Kilmarnock in 1786, Burns gives his reasons for writing:

> To amuse himself with the little creations of his own fancy, amid the toils and fatigues of a laborious life; to transcribe the various feelings, the loves, the griefs, the hopes, the fears, in his own breast; to find some kind of counterpoise to the struggles of a world, always an alien scene, a task uncouth to the poetical mind; these were his motives for courting the Muses, and in these he found Poetry to be its own reward.

Not only does Burns write for self amusement and 'to find some kind of counterpoise' he also writes out of a need for self-expression. His emphasis on emotion and sentiment, especially in song, anticipates Romantic literary practice, but he belongs to a mainstream eighteenth-century tradition in his devotion to accurate recording of what he sees. An example of this attention to detail comes not only in Burns's ability to give a sense of the physical world but also in his clear-sighted observations of himself, of his friends and enemies and of the surrounding environment. An early love song in this selection, 'Now westlin winds and slaught'ring guns' combines outrage at the cruelty of the 'slaught'ring guns' directed against game birds with the love of a man for a woman. Burns was definitely not of his generation in his opposition to blood sports. Man's abuse of power over nature's creatures matters to him as it does to the present generation. His distress at the accidental destruction of the mouse's home in 'To A Mouse' is real. In displacing the mouse he has broken the fragile bond of 'nature's social union'.

Two hundred years after Burns's death he is still as topical as ever in his approach to the environment. He loved Nature and the unspoilt, wild places he saw on his tours of Scotland. Burns wrote of them in such poems as 'Castle Gordon':

> Wildly here without control
> Nature reigns and rules the whole

> In that sober, pensive mood
> Dearest to the feeling soul
> She plants the forest, pours the flood

Burns loved running water. Consider, for instance, the song 'Flow gently, sweet Afton, among thy green braes', about which he comments:

> There is a small river, Afton, that falls into Nith, near New Cumnock, which has some charming, wild, romantic scenery on its banks. – I have a particular pleasure in those little pieces of poetry such as our Scots songs, &c. where the names and landskip features of rivers, lakes, or woodlands, that one knows, are introduced. I attempted a compliment of that kind, to Afton as follows.

Similarly, he is inspired to create 'Bonie lassie, will ye go, will ye go, will ye go?' under the birks or birches of Aberfeldy, at or near Moness, in Perthshire. Best known of all, probably, is his way of referring in his songs to the river he knew first in childhood, the Doon. In contrast, he refers to the sea less often than might seem likely today, considering its relative nearness to places in Ayrshire where he lived, beginning with Alloway. This has to do with the fact that the sea was not yet thought of by someone of Burns's social background in terms of attractive views or holidays. Despite this, Burns finds words which refer to the ocean, swearing loyalty in love for instance 'Till a' the seas gang dry, my dear'.

Burns is the outstanding song-writing poet of the western world. Song-writing was his lifelong pursuit and passion. Such popular love-songs as 'O, My love's like a red, red rose' ensure that his fame extends far beyond his native Scotland. 'A man's a man for a' that' boldly expresses global democratic ideals, while the Olympic Games and New Year remind us that 'Auld Lang Syne' is accepted universally as a song in celebration of friendship. Such individual songs belong to a total of 373 songs, an unsurpassed achievement. The chronological arrangement of the songs offers indisputable evidence of the range and quality of Burns's lyric inspiration. This extends from the early years in Ayrshire which produced such excellent songs as 'Corn Rigs' and 'Mary Morrison', and a masterpiece in the cantata 'Love And Liberty', to the later years of song-writing for James Johnson's *Scots Musical Museum*. Burns's skill and dedication made the *Museum* into Scotland's greatest song collection, studded with examples of his mature art, like 'It was a' for our rightfu' king', recalling the final Jacobite Rising, and, in quite different mood, 'Willie brew'd a peck o' maut', a drinking-song set to a tune by Burns's friend Alan Masterton. The songs were invariably conceived with particular tunes in mind, rather than as mere words on the page requiring melodies to express their full meaning. As this transforms possibilities for understanding, Burns emerges in his true light after two hundred years as a creative artist in more than one medium, the originator of a major aesthetic achievement. An interesting point about Burns as a creator of songs is that while on the one hand he is a master of words which achieve beautiful or comic simplicity, many of his modern admirers are far from confident about how to supply the music on which his songs depend. If music is different today, so also is understanding of Burns's words. Textual authority belongs to the written words as transmitted to us through manuscripts, *The Scots Musical Museum*, and other early collections of sources.

Key ideas for understanding Burns the writer are Song, Senti-ment, Satire and Scotland. Of these four, song and satire can be thought of as natural opposites, the first usually expressing praise, the second attack or criticism of ideas and attitudes Burns disliked. Tunes which the poet enjoyed and positive feelings – very often concerning 'love' or ardent affection – helped to inspire many of his songs. Strongly critical moods, on the other hand, led him to write scathing satires, like 'Holy Willie's Prayer' and a number of sardonically phrased songs as well. The basis of much of Burns's satiric writing is personal. He wrote, as he spoke, about individuals, whether or not he took the trouble to disguise their identity. This applies to 'Death And Doctor Hornbook', which is on one level a personal satire or lampoon on the character of 'Jock Hornbook', the apothecary and schoolmaster John Wilson, yet is also a poem mocking the idea of Death by robbing it of terror and solemnity.

He makes much use of Sentiment, especially in his songs, as the language of feeling valued in his time. But Sentiment does not always rule as an unloving song about the Act of Union of 1707, 'Fareweel to a' our Scottish Fame', shows. It expresses a sense of contempt for politicians who are portrayed as having let Scotland down.

Burns had command of different verse forms as early as 1786. This includes from the specifically Lowland Scottish verse tradition what became his best known metre, 'Standart Habbie', or the Burns stanza as it came to be called after his death. It takes its name from a comic elegy by the seventeenth-century Scottish poet Robert Sempill, 'The Life and Death of Habbie Simson, the Piper of Kilbarchan'. Burns widened the use of the six-line stanza beyond comic elegy and satire to include more serious poems such as 'The Vision', or to convey genuine grief as in his 'Elegy on Capt M—H—'. It is no accident that he mocks the Devil in his 'Address to the Deil' in this metre, nor that he should choose it for a virtuoso display of spoken Scots in 'The Auld Farmer's New-Year-Morning Salutation to his Auld Mare, Maggie'.

A love of his native land is clear in all his works, including his own favourite, 'Tam o' Shanter', a poem inspired near the River Nith a few miles from Dumfries by an exile's thoughts of Alloway and Ayrshire. Burns turns to advantage in his writings his journeys within Ayrshire and elsewhere in Scotland. He undertook tours to the Highlands and to the Borders which inspired him to write many fine poems and songs, including 'Blythe, blythe, and merry was she' and 'Killiecrankie'. In his last years in Dumfries in the Southwest of Scotland, he continued to praise the beauty and splendour of all Scotland.

DONALD A. LOW

# Robert Burns

# The Twa Dogs, A Tale

'Twas in that place o' Scotland's isle,
That bears the name o' auld king COIL,
And aft he's prest, and aft he ca's it guid;
The frugal Wifie, garrulous, will tell,
Upon a bonie day in June,
When wearing thro' the afternoon,
*Twa Dogs*, that were na thrang at hame,    busy
Forgather'd ance upon a time.

    The first I'll name, they ca'd him *Caesar*,
Was keepet for His Honor's pleasure;
His hair, his size, his mouth, his lugs,    ears
10  Shew'd he was nane o' Scotland's dogs,
But whalpet some place far abroad,    whelped
Where sailors gang to fish for Cod.

    His locked, letter'd, braw brass-collar
Shew'd him the *gentleman* an' *scholar*;
But tho' he was o' high degree,
The fient a pride na pride had he,    not a bit of
But wad hae spent an hour caressan,
Ev'n wi' a Tinkler-gipsey's *messan*:    mongrel
At Kirk or Market, Mill or Smiddie,    church, smithy
20  Nae tawted *tyke*, tho' e'er sae duddie,    matted cur, ragged
But he wad stan't, as glad to see him,    stood
An' stroan't on stanes an' hillocks wi' him.    watered, stones

    The tither was a *ploughman's collie*,
A rhyming, ranting, raving billie,    merry, fellow
Wha for his friend an' comrade had him,
And in his freaks had *Luath* ca'd him,    odd notions
After some dog in[1] *Highland sang*,
Was made lang syne, lord knows how lang.    long ago

---

[1] Cuchullin's dog in Ossian's Fingal.

He was a gash an' faithfu' *tyke*,                    wise, dog
30  As ever lap a sheugh or dyke.                     leapt, ditch, stone wall
His honest, sonsie, baws'nt face                      pleasant, white-striped
Ay gat him friends in ilka place;
His breast was white, his towzie back,                shaggy
Weel clad wi' coat o' glossy black;
His gawsie tail, wi' upward curl,                     cheerful
Hung owre his hurdies wi' a swirl.                    buttocks

Nae doubt but they were fain o' ither,                fond of
An' unco pack an' thick thegither;                    very intimate together
Wi' social nose whyles snuff'd an' snowket;           sniffed, poked about
40  Whyles mice and modewurks they howket;            moles, dug
Whyles scour'd awa in lang excursion,                 ranged
An' worry'd ither in diversion;
Till tir'd at last wi' mony a farce,
They set them down upon their arse,
An' there began a lang digression
About the *lords o' the creation*.

## CAESAR

I've aften wonder'd, honest *Luath*,
What sort o' life poor dogs like you have;
An' when the *gentry's* life I saw,
50  What way *poor bodies* liv'd ava.                 folk, at all

Our *Laird* gets in his racked rents,
His coals, his kane, an' a' his stents:               payment in kind, dues
He rises when he likes himsel;
His flunkies answer at the bell;
He ca's his coach; he ca's his horse;
He draws a bonie, silken purse
As lang's my tail, where thro' the steeks,            stitches
The yellow letter'd *Geordie* keeks.                  guinea, peeps

Frae morn to een it's nought but toiling,             evening
60  At baking, roasting, frying, boiling;

An' tho' the gentry first are steghan,    *cramming*
Yet ev'n the *ha' folk* fill their peghan    *servants, stomach*
Wi' sauce, ragouts, an' sic like trashtrie,    *trash*
That's little short o' downright wastrie.    *waste/extravagance*
Our *Whipper-in*, wee, blastet wonner,    *hunt-servant, wonder*
Poor worthless elf, it eats a dinner,
Better than ony *Tenant-man*
His Honor has in a' the lan':
An' what poor *Cot-folk* pit their painch in,    *cottagers, put, paunch*
70 I own it's past my comprehension.

### LUATH

Trowth, Caesar, whyles they're fash't    *indeed, troubled*
    enough;
A *Cotter* howkan in a sheugh,
Wi' dirty stanes biggan a dyke.    *building*
Bairan a quarry, an' sic like,    *clearing*
Himsel, a wife, he thus sustains
A smytrie o' wee, duddie weans,    *swarm, children*
An' nought but his han'-daurk, to keep    *labour of his hands*
Them right an' tight in thack an' raep.    *thatch and rope*

An' when they meet wi' sair disasters,    *sore*
80 Like loss o' health or want o' masters,
Ye maist wad think, a wee touch langer,
An' they maun starve o' cauld and hunger:
But how it comes, I never kent yet,
They're maistly wonderfu' contented;
An' buirdly chiels, and clever hizzies,    *well-built lads,*
Are bred in sic a way as this is.    *wenches*

### CAESAR

But then, to see how ye're negleket,
How huff'd, an' cuff'd, an' disrespeket!    *scolded*
L—d man, our gentry care as little
90 For *delvers*, *ditchers*, an' sic cattle;    *beasts*
They gang as saucy by poor folk,
As I wad by a stinkan brock.    *badger*

    I've notic'd, on our Laird's *court-day*,    rent-day
An' mony a time my heart's been wae,    sad
Poor *tenant bodies*, scant o' cash,
How they maun thole a *factor's* snash;    endure, insolence
He'll stamp an' threaten, curse an' swear,
He'll *apprehend* them, *poind* their gear;    seize, distrain
While they maun stan', wi' aspect humble,
100  An' hear it a', an' fear an' tremble!

    I see how folk live that hae riches;
But surely poor-folk maun be wretches!

### LUATH

    They're no sae wretched's ane wad think;    as one would
Tho' constantly on poortith's brink,    poverty
They're sae accustom'd wi' the sight,
The view o't gies them little fright.

    Then chance and fortune are sae guided,
They're ay in less or mair provided;
And tho' fatigu'd wi' close employment,
110  A blink o' rest's a sweet enjoyment.

    The dearest comfort o' their lives,
Their grushie weans an faithfu' wives;    thriving
The *prattling things* are just their pride,
That sweetens a' their fire side.

    An' whyles twalpennie-worth o' *nappy*    twelvepenny, ale
Can mak the bodies unco happy;    folk
They lay aside their private cares,
To mind the Kirk and State affairs;
They'll talk o' *patronage* an' *priests*,
120  Wi' kindling fury i' their breasts,
Or tell what new taxation's comin,
An' ferlie at the folk in LON'ON.    marvel

As bleak-fac'd Hallowmass returns,
They get the jovial, rantan *Kirns*,  *harvest-homes*
When *rural life*, of ev'ry station,
Unite in common recreation;
Love blinks, Wit slaps, an' social Mirth
Forgets there's *care* upo' the earth.

That *merry day* the year begins,
130 They bar the door on frosty win's;
The nappy reeks wi' mantling ream,  *smokes, foam*
An' sheds a heart-inspiring steam;
The luntan pipe, an' sneeshin mill,  *smoking, snuff-box*
Are handed round wi' right guid will;
The cantie, auld folks, crackan crouse,  *lively, talking cheerfully*
The young anes rantan thro' the house –  *romping*
My heart has been sae fain to see them,  *glad*
That I for joy hae barket wi' them.

Still it's owre true that ye hae said,
140 Sic game is now owre aften play'd;  *often*
There's monie a creditable *stock*
O' decent, honest, fawsont folk,  *respectable*
Are riven out baith root an' branch,  *torn*
Some rascal's pridefu' greed to quench,
Wha thinks to knit himsel the faster
In favor wi' some *gentle Master*,
Wha aiblins thrang a *parliamentin*,  *perhaps*
For Britain's guid his saul indentin –  *soul, pledging*

CAESAR

Haith lad ye little ken about it;  *'a petty oath' (B)*
150 *For Britain's guid*! guid faith! I doubt it.
Say rather, gaun as PREMIERS lead him,  *going*
An' saying *aye* or *no's* they bid him:
At Operas an' Plays parading,
Mortgaging, gambling, masquerading:
Or maybe, in a frolic daft,
To HAGUE or CALAIS takes a waft,  *sea-trip*

To make a *tour* an' tak a whirl,                     go on the Grand Tour
To learn *bon ton* an' see the worl'.

There, at VIENNA or VERSAILLES,
160  He rives his father's auld entails;               splits, estate succession
Or by MADRID he takes the rout,                       road
To thrum *guittars* an' fecht wi' nowt;               fight, cattle
Or down *Italian Vista* startles,
Wh-re-hunting amang groves o' myrtles:
Then bowses drumlie *German-water*,                   boozes, cloudy
To mak himsel look fair and fatter,
An' purge the bitter ga's an' cankers,                galls
O' curst *Venetian* b-res an' ch-ncres.               cracks, ulcers

*For Britain's guid*! for her destruction!
170  Wi' dissipation, feud an' faction!

LUATH

Hech man! dear sirs! is that the gate,                way
They waste sae mony a braw estate!
Are we sae foughten and harass'd                      worn out
For gear to gang that gate at last!                   wealth

O would they stay aback frae courts,
An' please themsels wi' countra sports,
It wad for ev'ry ane be better,
The *Laird*, the *Tenant*, an' the *Cotter*!
For thae frank, rantan, ramblan billies,             these
180  Fient haet o' them's ill hearted fellows;        not one
Except for breakin o' their timmer,                   timber
Or speakin lightly o' their *Limmer*,                 mistress
Or shootin of a hare or moorcock,
The ne'er-a-bit they're ill to poor folk.            not in the least

But will ye tell me, master *Caesar*,
Sure *great folk*'s life's a life o' pleasure?
Nae cauld nor hunger e'er can steer them,             affect
The vera thought o't need na fear them.               frighten

CAESAR

L—d man, were ye but whyles where I am,
190 The *gentles* ye wad ne'er envy them!    'great folks' (B)

It's true, they need na starve or sweat,
Thro' Winter's cauld, or Summer's heat;
They've nae sair-wark to craze their banes,    hard work, bones
An' fill *auld-age* wi' grips an' granes;    gripes and groans
But *human-bodies* are sic fools,
For a' their colledges an' schools,
That when nae *real* ills perplex them,
They *mak* enow themsels to vex them;    enough
An' ay the less they hae to sturt them,    trouble
200 In like proportion, less will hurt them.

A country fellow at the pleugh,    plough
His *acre's* till'd, he's right eneugh;
A country girl at her wheel,
Her *dizzen's* done, she's unco weel;    dozen cuts of yarn
But Gentlemen, an' Ladies warst,    worst of all
Wi' ev'n down *want o'wark* are curst.    sheer lack of work
They loiter, lounging, lank an' lazy;
Tho' deil-haet ails them, yet uneasy;    damn-all
Their days, insipid, dull an' tasteless,
210 Their nights, unquiet, lang an' restless.

An ev'n their sports, their balls an' races,
Their galloping thro' public places,
There's sic parade, sic pomp an' art,
The joy can scarcely reach the heart.

The *Men* cast out in *party-matches*,    fall out, card-contests
Then sowther a' in deep debauches.
Ae night, they're mad wi' drink an' wh-ring,
Niest day their life is past enduring.    next

The *Ladies* arm-in-arm in clusters,
220 As great an' gracious a' as sisters;
But hear their *absent thoughts* o' ither,
They're a' run deils an' jads thegither.    all complete hussies

Whyles, owre the wee bit cup an' platie,
They sip the *scandal-potion* pretty;
Or lee-lang nights, wi' crabbet leuks,          live-long, cross looks
Por owre the devil's *pictur'd beuks*;          playing-cards
Stake on a chance a farmer's stackyard,
An' cheat like ony *unhang'd blackguard*.

There's some exceptions, man an' woman;
230   But this is Gentry's life in common.

By this, the sun was out o' sight,
An' darker gloamin brought the night:           twilight
The *bum-clock* humm'd wi' lazy drone,          beetle
The kye stood rowtan i' the loan;               cattle, lowing, pasture
When up they gat an' shook their lugs,
Rejoic'd they were na *men* but *dogs*;
And each took off his several way,
Resolv'd to meet some ither day.

# Scotch Drink

*Gie him strong* Drink *until he wink,*
*    That's sinking in despair;*
*An'* liquor *guid to fire his bluid,*
*    That's prest wi' grief an' care:*
*There let him bowse an' deep carouse,*
*    Wi' bumpers flowing o'er,*
*Till he forgets his* loves *or* debts
*    An' minds his griefs no more.*
Solomon's Proverbs, xxxi. 6, 7

Let other Poets raise a fracas
'Bout vines, an' wines, an' drunken *Bacchus*,  drunken
An' crabbed names an' stories wrack us,         ill-natured
        An' grate our lug,                      ear
I sing the juice *Scotch bear* can mak us,      barley
        In glass or jug.

O thou, my MUSE! guid, auld SCOTCH-DRINK!
Whether thro' wimplin worms thou jink,  *twisting tubes, slip fast*
Or, richly brown, ream owre the brink,  *froth*
      In glorious faem,  *foam*
10
Inspire me, till I *lisp* an' *wink*,
      To sing thy name!

Let husky Wheat the haughs adorn,  *level land by a river*
And Aits set up their awnie horn,  *oats, bearded*
An' Pease an' Beans, at een or morn,  *evening*
      Perfume the plain,
Leeze me on thee *John Barleycorn*,  *you delight me*
      Thou king o'grain!

On thee aft Scotland chows her cood,  *chews, cud*
20
In souple scones, the wale o' food!  *pliable, choice*
Or tumbling in the boiling flood
      Wi' kail an' beef;  *vegetable broth*
But when thou pours thy strong *heart's blood*,
      There thou shines chief.

Food fills the wame, an' keeps us livin;  *stomach*
Tho' life's a gift no worth receivin,
When heavy-dragg'd wi' pine an' grievin;
      But oil'd by thee,
The wheels o' life gae down-hill, scrievin,  *gliding swiftly*
30
      Wi' rattlin glee.

Thou chears the head o' doited Lear;  *stupefied learning*
Thou chears the heart o' drooping Care;
Thou strings the nerves o' Labor-sair,  *-hard*
      At's weary toil;
Thou ev'n brightens dark Despair,
      Wi' gloomy smile.

Aft, clad in massy, siller weed,  *silver dress*
Wi' Gentles thou erects thy head;  *'great folks' (B)*
Yet humbly kind, in time o' need,
40
      The *poor man's* wine;

His wee drap pirratch, or his bread,     drop of, porridge
       Thou kitchens fine.     seasons

Thou art the life o' public haunts;
But thee, what were our fairs and rants?     without, sprees
Ev'n godly meetings o' the saunts,     saints/'the elect'
       By thee inspir'd,
When gaping they besiege the *tents*,     'field pulpit' (B)
       Are doubly fir'd.

That *merry night* we get the corn in,
50   O sweetly, then, thou reams the horn in!     horn vessel
Or reekan on a *New-year-mornin*     smoking
       In cog or bicker,     wooden drinking cups
An' just a wee drap *sp'ritual burn* in,     water used in brewing
       An gusty sucker!     tasty sugar

When Vulcan gies his bellys breath,
An' Ploughmen gather wi' their graith,     ploughing gear
O rare! to see thee fizz an' freath     froth
       I' the lugget caup!     wood-dish with handles
Then *Burnewin* comes on like Death     'burn-wind'/blacksmith
60       At ev'ry chap.     stroke

Nae mercy, then, for airn or steel;     iron
The brawnie, banie, ploughman-chiel     bony, -lad
Brings hard owrehip, wi' sturdy wheel,     over the hip
       The strong forehammer,     sledge-hammer
Till block an' studdie ring an' reel     anvil
       Wi' dinsome clamour.     noisy

When skirlin weanies see the light,     yelling infants
Thou maks the gossips clatter bright,     neighbour-women chatter
How fumbling coofs their dearies slight,     clowns
70       Wae worth them for't!     cursed be
While healths gae round to him wha, *tight*,     virile
       Gies famous sport.     gives

When neebors anger at a plea,                    neighbours
An' just as wud as wud can be,                   angry
How easy can the *barley-brie*                   whisky
     Cement the quarrel!
It's aye the cheapest Lawyer's fee
     To taste the barrel.

Alake! that e'er my *Muse* has reason,
80 To wyte her countrymen wi' treason!            blame
But monie daily weet their weason                wet, gullet
     Wi' liquors nice,
An' hardly, in a winter season,
     E'er spier her price.                  ask

Wae worth that *Brandy*, burnan trash!
Fell source o' monie a pain an' brash!           severe, illness
Twins monie a poor, doylt, druken hash           deprives, muddled,
     O' half his days;                     drunken waster
An' sends, beside, auld *Scotland's* cash
90      To her warst faes.                worst foes

Ye Scots wha wish auld Scotland well,
Ye chief, to you my tale I tell,
Poor, plackless devils like *mysel*,             penniless
     It sets you ill,
Wi' bitter, dearthfu' *wines* to mell,           meddle
     Or foreign gill.                      measure

May *Gravels* round his blather wrench,          urinary pains, bladder
An' *Gouts* torment him, inch by inch,
Wha twists his gruntle wi' a glunch              snout, frown
100      O' sour disdain,
Out owre a glass o' *Whisky-punch*
     Wi' honest men!

O *Whisky*! soul o' plays an' pranks!
Accept a *Bardie's* gratefu' thanks!             poet's

When wanting thee, what tuneless cranks          noises
      Are my poor Verses!
Thou comes – they rattle i' their ranks
      At ither's arses!

Thee *Ferintosh*! O sadly lost!                  a whisky
110 Scotland lament frae coast to coast!
Now colic-grips, an' barkin hoast,               cough
      May kill us a';
Fo loyal Forbes' *Charter'd boast*
      Is ta'en awa!

Thae curst horse-leeches o' th'Excise,           those
Wha mak the *Whisky stells* their prize!         stills
Haud up thy han' *Diel*! ance, twice, *thrice*!  hold, Devil
      There, seize the blinkers!   spies/cheats
An' bake them up in brunstane pies               brimstone
120       For poor d—n'd *Drinkers*.

*Fortune*, if thou'll but gie me still           give
Hale breeks, a scone, an' *whisky gill*,         intact breeches
An' rowth o' *rhyme* to rave at will,            abundance
      Tak a' the rest,
An' deal't about as thy blind skill
      Directs thee best.

# The Holy Fair

*A robe of seeming truth and trust*
  *Hid crafty observation;*
*And secret hung, with poison'd crust,*
  *The dirk of Defamation:*
*A mask that like the gorget show'd,*
  *Dye-varying, on the pigeon;*
*And for a mantle large and broad,*
  *He wrapt him in Religion.*
                Hypocrisy A-La-Mode

### I

Upon a simmer Sunday morn,                    summer
  When Nature's face is fair,
I walked forth to view the corn,
  An' snuff the callor air.                    sniff, fresh
The rising sun, owre GALSTON Muirs,                    over
  Wi' glorious light was glintan;
The hares were hirplan down the furrs,                    moving unevenly
                                         forward, furrows
  The lav'rocks they were chantan                    larks
        Fu' sweet that day.                    very

### II

10 As lightsomely I glowr'd abroad                    gazed intently
  To see a scene sae gay,
Three *hizzies*, early at the road,                    wenches
  Cam skelpan up the way.                    hurrying
Twa had manteeles o' dolefu' black,                    capes
  But ane wi' lyart lining;                    grey
The third, that gaed a wee a-back,                    a little in the rear
  Was in the fashion shining
        Fu' gay that day.

### III

The *twa* appear'd like sisters twin,
20   In feature, form an' claes;                    clothes
Their visage wither'd, lang an' thin,
  An' sour as ony slaes:                    sloes
The *third* cam up, hap-step-an'-loup,                    hop-step-and-jump
  As light as ony lambie,                    little lamb
An' wi' a curchie low did stoop,                    curtsy
  As soon as e'er she saw me,
        Fu' kind that day.

### IV

Wi' bonnet aff, quoth I, 'Sweet lass,
  I think ye seem to ken me;
30 I'm sure I've seen that bonie face,
  But yet I canna name ye.'
Quo' she, an' laughan as she spak,                    said, spoke
  An' taks me by the han's,                    hands

'Ye, for my sake, hae gien the feck            have given most
    Of a' the *ten comman's*                 commandments
        A screed some day.'              tear/rent


### V

'My name is FUN – your cronie dear,
    The nearest friend ye hae;
An' this is SUPERSTITION here,
40    An' that's HYPOCRISY.
I'm gaun to \*\*\*\*\*\*\*\*\* *holy fair*,          [Mauchline]
    To spend an hour in daffin:                frolic
Gin ye'll go there, yon runkl'd pair,          if, that wrinkled
    We will get famous laughin
        At them this day.'


### VI

Quoth I, 'With a' my heart, I'll do't;
    I'll get my Sunday's sark on,               shirt
An' meet you on the holy spot;
    Faith, we'se hae fine remarkin!'            we'll, entertainment
50 Then I gaed hame at crowdie-time,             breakfast-time
    An' soon I made me ready;
For roads were clad, frae side to side,
    Wi' monie a wearie body,                    person
        In droves that day.


### VII

Here, farmers gash, in ridin graith,           smart, habit
    Gaed hoddan by their cotters;               jogging, cottagers
There, swankies young, in braw braid-claith,   strapping lads, broad-
    Are springan owre the gutters.              cloth
The lasses, skelpan barefit, thrang,           hurrying, barefoot in a
60    In silks an' scarlets glitter;          crowd
Wi' *sweet-milk cheese*, in monie a whang,     thick slice
    An' *farls*, bak'd wi' butter,              bits of oaten bannock
        Fu' crump that day.             'hard and brittle' (B)


### VIII

When by the *plate* we set our nose,
    Weel heaped up wi' ha'pence,

A greedy glowr *Black-bonnet* throws,
    An' we maun draw our tippence.      twopence
Then in we go to see the show,
    On ev'ry side they're gath'ran;
70 Some carryan dails, some chairs an' stools,    deal planks
    An' some are busy bleth'ran      chatting hard
        Right loud that day.

### IX

Here stands a shed to fend the show'rs,
    An' screen our countra Gentry;
There, *Racer Jess*, an' twathree-wh-res,    two or three
    Are blinkan at the entry.
Here sits a raw o' tittlan jads,    row, gossiping hussies
    Wi' heaving breasts an' bare neck;
An' there, a batch o' *Wabster lads*,    weaver
80     Blackguarding frae K\*\*\*\*\*\*\*ck    roistering, [Kilmarnock]
        For *fun* this day.

### X

Here, some are thinkan on their sins,
    An' some upo' their claes;
Ane curses feet that fyl'd his shins,    fouled
    Anither sighs an' prays:
On this hand sits an *Elect* swatch,    sample
    Wi' screw'd-up, grace-proud faces;    sanctimonious
On that, a set o' chaps, at watch,
    Thrang winkan on the lasses    throng
90         To *chairs* that day.

### XI

O happy is that man, an' blest!
    Nae wonder that it pride him!
Whase ain dear lass, that he likes best,    own
    Comes clinkan down beside him!    sitting smartly
Wi' arm repos'd on the *chair-back*,
    He sweetly does compose him;
Which, by degrees, slips round her *neck*
    An's loof upon her *bosom*    palm
        Unkend that day.

### XII

100 Now a' the congregation o'er
    Is silent expectation;
For ****** speels the holy door,                    [Moodie] climbs
    Wi' tidings o' s-lv-t—n.
Should *Hornie*, as in ancient days,                Satan
    'Mang sons o' G— present him,
The vera sight o' ******'s face,
    To's ain *het hame* had sent him               hot home (Hell)
        Wi' fright that day.

### XIII

Hear how he clears the points o' Faith
110     Wi' rattlin an' thumpin!
Now meekly calm, now wild in wrath,
    He's stampan, an' he's jumpan!
His lengthen'd chin, his turn'd up snout,
    His *eldritch* squeel an' gestures,             hideous
O how they fire the heart devout,
    Like *cantharidian* plaisters
        On sic a day!

### XIV

But hark! the *tent* has chang'd its voice;         'field pulpit' (B)
    There's peace an' rest nae langer;
120 For a' the *real judges* rise,
    They canna sit for anger.
***** opens out his cauld harangues,                [Smith]
    *On practice* and on *morals*,
An' aff the *godly* pour in thrangs,
    To gie the jars an' barrels
        A lift that day.

### XV

What signifies his barren shine,
    Of *moral pow'rs* an' *reason*?
His English style, an' gesture fine,
130     Are a' clean out o' season.
Like SOCRATES or ANTONINE,

Or some auld pagan heathen,
The *moral man* he does define,
But ne'er a word o' *faith* in
     That's right that day.

### XVI

In guid time comes an antidote
  Against sic poosion'd nostrum;     poisoned remedy
For *******, frae the water-fit,     [Peebles], river-mouth
  Ascends the *holy rostrum*:
140 See, up he's got the word o' G—,
  An' meek an' mim has view'd it,     demure
While COMMON-SENSE has taen the road,
  An' aff, an' up the *Cowgate*
     Fast, fast that day.

### XVII

Wee ****** niest the Guard relieves,     [Miller], next
  An' Orthodoxy raibles,     gabbles
Tho' in his heart he weel believes,
  An' thinks it auld wives' fables:
But faith! the birkie wants a *Manse*,     fellow
150 So, cannilie he hums them;     dextrously, takes them in
Altho' his *carnal* Wit an' Sense
  Like hafflins-wise o'ercomes him     in half measure/partly
     At times that day.

### XVIII

Now, butt an' ben, the Change-house fills,     in outer and inner room, tavern
  Wi' *yill-caup* Commentators:     ale-cup
Here's crying out for bakes an' gills,     biscuits, drams
  An' there the pint-stowp clatters;     -measure
While thick an' thrang, an' loud an' lang,     closely engaged together
  Wi' *Logic*, an' wi' *Scripture*,
160 They raise a din, that, in the end,
  Is like to breed a rupture
     O' wrath that day.

### XIX

Leeze me on Drink! it gies us mair                    I'm all for
   Than either School or Colledge:
It kindles Wit, it waukens Lear,                      wakens Learning
   It pangs us fou o' Knowledge.             stuffs, full
Be't *whisky-gill* or *penny-wheep*,                 small beer
   Or ony stronger potion,
It never fails, on drinkin deep,
170    To kittle up our *notion*,           rouse, fancy
      By night or day.

### XX

The lads an' lasses, blythely bent
   To mind baith *saul* an' *body*,          soul
Sit round the table, weel content,
   An' steer about the *toddy*.               whisky, hot water and sugar
On this ane's dress, an' that ane's leuk,            expression
   They're makin observations;
While some are cozie i' the neuk,                    corner
   An' forming *assignations*
180      To meet some day.

### XXI

But now the L—'s ain trumpet touts,                  blasts
   Till a' the hills are rairan,              roaring
An' echoes back return the shouts;
   Black ****** is na spairan:                [Russel], sparing
His piercin words, like Highlan swords,
   Divide the joints an' marrow;
His talk o' H-ll, where devils dwell,
   Our vera[1] 'Sauls does harrow'
      Wi' fright that day!

### XXII

190  A vast, unbottom'd, boundless *Pit*,
   Fill'd fou o' *lowan brunstane*,           blazing brimstone
Whase raging flame, an' scorching heat,
   Wad melt the hardest whun-stane!           whinstone
The *half asleep* start up wi' fear,
   An' think they hear it roaran,
When presently it does appear,

---

[1] Shakespeare's Hamlet.

'Twas but some neebor *snoran*     neighbour snoring
    Asleep that day.

### XXIII

    'Twad be owre lang a tale to tell,
200    How monie stories past,
    An' how they crouded to the yill,     crowded, ale
    When they were a' dismist:
How drink gaed round, in cogs an' caups,    dishes, bowls
    Amang the furms an' benches;    forms
An' *cheese* an' *bread*, frae women's laps,
    Was dealt about in lunches,
        An' dawds that day.    hunks

### XXIV

In comes a gawsie, gash *Guidwife*,    jovial, neat matron
    An' sits down by the fire,
210  Syne draws her *kebbuk* an' her knife;    then, cheese
    The lasses they are shyer.
The auld *Guidmen*, about the *grace*,    husbands
    Frae side to side they bother,
Till some ane by his bonnet lays,
    An' gies them't, like a *tether*,    rope
        Fu' lang that day.    very

### XXV

Waesucks! for him that gets nae lass,    alas
    Or lasses that hae naething!
Sma' need has he to say a grace,
220  Or melvie his braw claithing!    'soil with meal' (B)
                      clothing
O *Wives* be mindfu', ance yoursel,
    How bonie lads ye wanted,
An' dinna, for a *kebbuck-heel*,    do not, heel of cheese
    Let lasses be affronted
        On sic a day!

### XXVI

Now *Clinkumbell*, wi' rattlan tow,    bellringer, rope
    Begins to jow an' croon;    toll and sound
Some swagger hame, the best they dow,    are able

Some wait the afternoon.
230 At slaps the billies halt a blink,                    gaps in dyke, fellows
  Till lasses strip their shoon:                         shoes
Wi' *faith* an' *hope*, an' *love* an' *drink*,
  They're a' in famous tune
        For crack that day.                              chat

### XXVII

How monie hearts this day converts,
  O' sinners and o' Lasses!
Their hearts o' stane, gin night are gane,              stone, by nightfall gone
  As saft as ony flesh is.                              soft
There's some are fou o' *love divine*;
240  There's some are fou o' *brandy*;
An' monie jobs that day begin,                          intrigues
  May end in *Houghmagandie*                            fornication
        Some ither day.

# Address to the Deil

*O Prince, O chief of many throned pow'rs,*
*That led th'embattl'd Seraphim to war –*

                    Milton

O Thou, whatever title suit thee!
Auld Hornie, Satan, Nick, or Clootie,                  Cloven-hoof
Wha in yon cavern grim an' sootie,
  Clos'd under hatches,
Spairges about the brunstane cootie,                   bespatters, brimstone
        To scaud poor wretches!                         tub
                                                        scald

Hear me, *auld Hangie*, for a wee,                     Hangman
An' let poor, *damned bodies* bee;
I'm sure sma' pleasure it can gie,
10        Ev'n to a *deil*,                             devil

To skelp an' scaud poor dogs like me,      smack
        An' hear us squeel!

Great is thy pow'r, an' great thy fame;
Far kend an' noted is thy name;
An' tho' yon *lowan heugh's* thy hame,      blazing pit
        Thou travels far;
An' faith! thou's neither lag nor lame,      backward
        Nor blate nor scaur.      bashful, afraid

Whyles, ranging like a roaran lion,
20  For prey, a' holes an' corners tryin;
Whyles, on the strong-wing'd Tempest flyin,
        Tirlan the *kirks*;      uncovering, churches
Whyles, in the human bosom pryin,
        Unseen thou lurks.

I've heard my rev'rend *Graunie* say,      grandmother
In lanely glens ye like to stray;      lonely
Or where auld, ruin'd castles, gray,
        Nod to the moon,
Ye fright the nightly wand'rer's way,
30          Wi' eldritch croon.      unearthly moan

When twilight did my *Graunie* summon,
To say her pray'rs, douse, honest woman!      sober
Aft 'yont the dyke she's heard you bumman,      behind, wall, humming
        Wi' eerie drone;
Or, rustling, thro' the boortries coman,      elder trees
        Wi' heavy groan.

Ae dreary, windy, winter night,
The stars shot down wi' sklentan light,      slanting
Wi' you, *mysel*, I gat a fright,
40          Ayont the lough;      beyond, loch
Ye, like a *rash-buss*, stood in sight,      clump of rushes
        Wi' waving sugh.      sound of wind

The cudgel in my neive did shake,      fist
Each bristl'd hair stood like a stake,

When wi' an eldritch, stoor *quaick, quaick*,          harsh
      Amang the springs,
Awa ye squatter'd like a *drake*,          'flutter in water' (B)
      On whistling wings.

Let *Warlocks* grim, an' wither'd *Hags*,
50 Tell how wi' you on ragweed nags,          ragwort
They skim the muirs an' dizzy crags,          moors
      Wi' wicked speed;
And in kirk-yards renew their leagues,
      Owre howcket dead.          exhumed

Thence, countra wives, wi' toil an' pain,
May plunge an' plunge the *kirn* in vain;          churn
For Oh! the yellow treasure's taen
      By witching skill;
An' dawtet, twal-pint *Hawkie's* gane          spoiled, twelve-cow
60       As yell's the Bill.          milkless as, bull

Thence, mystic knots mak great abuse,
On *Young-Guidmen*, fond, keen an' croose;          -husbands, confident
When the best *wark-lume* i' the house,          work-loom
      By cantraip wit,          magic
Is instant made no worth a louse,
      Just at the bit.          critical moment

When thowes dissolve the snawy hoord,          thaws, snowy drift
An' float the jinglan icy boord,          (on), cracking, surface
Then, *Water-kelpies* haunt the foord,          waterhorse demons,
70       By your direction,          ford
An' nighted Trav'llers are allur'd
      To their destruction.

An' aft your moss-traversing *Spunkies*          wills o' the wisp
Decoy the wight that late an' drunk is:
The bleezan, curst, mischievous monkies          blazing
      Delude his eyes,
Till in some miry slough he sunk is,
      Ne'er mair to rise.

When MASONS' mystic *word* an' *grip*,
80    In storms an' tempests raise you up,
Some cock or cat, your rage maun stop,
   Or, strange to tell!
The *youngest Brother* ye wad whip
   Aff straught to *H-ll*.   straight

Lang syne in EDEN's bonie yard,  long ago, garden
When youthfu' lovers first were pair'd,
An' all the Soul of Love they shar'd,
   The raptur'd hour,
Sweet on the fragrant, flow'ry swaird,  sward
90       In shady bow'r.

Then you, ye auld, snick-drawing dog!  latch-
Ye cam to Paradise incog,  unknown
An' play'd on man a cursed brogue,  trick
   (Black be your fa'!)
An' gied the infant warld a shog,  world, shock
   'Maist ruin'd a'.

D'ye mind that day, when in a bizz,  remember, stir
Wi' reeket duds, an' reestet gizz,  smoky clothes, 'cured' wig
Ye did present your smoutie phiz,  ugly face
100       'Mang better folk,
An' sklented on the *man of Uzz*,  directed aslant
   Your spitefu' joke?

An how ye gat him i' your thrall,
An' brak him out o' house an' hal',
While scabs an' botches did him gall,  'angry tumours' (B)
   Wi' bitter claw,  scratching
An' lows'd his ill-tongu'd, wicked *Scawl*  loosed, abusive woman
   Was warst ava?  worst of all

But a' your doings to rehearse,
110    Your wily snares an' fechtin fierce,  fighting
Sin' that day[1] MICHAEL did you pierce,

---

[1] Vide Milton, Book 6th.

> Down to this time,
> Wad ding a' *Lallan* tongue, or *Erse*,     weary, Lowland, Gaelic
> In Prose or Rhyme.

> An' now, auld *Cloots*, I ken ye're thinkan,
> A certain *Bardie's* rantin, drinkin,     poet
> Some luckless hour will send him linkan,     going briskly
> To your black pit;
> But faith! he'll turn a corner jinkan,     side-stepping
> 120    An' cheat you yet.

> But fare-you-weel, auld *Nickie-ben*!
> O wad ye tak a thought an' men'!     an mend
> Ye aiblins might – I dinna ken –     perhaps
> Still hae a *stake* –     chance
> I'm wae to think upo' yon den,     unhappy
> Ev'n for your sake!

# The Death and Dying Words of Poor Mailie,

### The Author's Only Pet Yowe, An Unco Mournfu' Tale

> As MAILIE, an' her lambs thegither,
> Was ae day nibbling on the tether,
> Upon her cloot she coost a hitch,     hoof, cast
> An' owre she warsl'd in the ditch:     struggled
> There, groaning, dying, she did ly,
> When[1] *Hughoc* he cam doytan by.     blundering

> Wi' glowrin een, an' lifted han's,     eyes, hands
> Poor *Hughoc* like a statue stan's;
> He saw her days were near hand ended,     almost

[1] A neebor herd-callan.

10   But, waes my heart! he could na mend it!          woe is
     He gaped wide, but naething spak,                 spoke
     At length poor *Mailie* silence brak.             broke

     'O thou, whase lamentable face
     Appears to mourn my woefu' case!
     My *dying words* attentive hear,
     An' bear them to my *Master* dear.

     'Tell him, if e'er again he keep
     As muckle gear as buy a *sheep*,                  money
     O, bid him never tye them mair,
20   Wi' wicked strings o' hemp or hair!
     But ca' them out to park or hill,
     An' let them wander at their will:
     So, may his flock increase an' grow
     To *scores* o' lambs, an' *packs* of woo'!        wool

     'Tell him, he was a Master kin',                  kindly
     An' ay was guid to me an' mine;
     An' now my *dying* charge I gie him,
     My helpless *lambs*, I trust them wi' him.

     'O, bid him save their harmless lives,
30   Frae dogs an' tods, an' butchers' knives!         foxes
     But gie them guid *cow-milk* their fill,
     Till they be fit to fend themsel;
     An' tent them duely, e'en an' morn,               tend
     Wi' taets o' *hay* an' ripps o' *corn*.           tufts, handfuls

     'An' may they never learn the gaets,              ways
     Of ither vile, wanrestfu' *Pets*!                 restless
     To slink thro' slaps, an' reave an' steal,        gaps, plunder
     At stacks o' pease, or stocks o' kail.            green kale
     So may they, like their great *forbears*,
40   For monie a year come thro' the sheers:
     So *wives* will gie them bits o' bread,
     An' *bairns* greet for them when they're dead.    weep

     'My poor *toop-lamb*, my son an' heir,            ram-

O, bid him breed him up wi' care!
An' if he live to be a beast,
To pit some havins in his breast!                    put, sense
An' warn him ay at riding time,
To stay content wi' *yowes* at hame;
An' no to rin an' wear his cloots,                   run, hooves
50    Like ither menseless, graceless brutes.        ill-bred, senseless

'An' niest my *yowie*, silly thing,                  next, young ewe
Gude keep thee frae a *tether string*!
O, may thou ne'er forgather up,
Wi' onie blastet, moorlan *toop*;                    accursed, ram
But ay keep mind to moop an' mell,                   nibble, mix
Wi' sheep o' credit like thysel!

'And now, *my bairns*, wi' my last breath,
I lea'e my blessin wi' you baith:
An' when ye think upo' your Mither,                  mother
60    Mind to be kind to ane anither.                remember

'Now, honest Hughoc, dinna fail,                     don't
To tell my Master a' my tale;
An' bid him burn this cursed *tether*,
An' for thy pains thou'se get my blather.'           you will, bladder

This said, poor *Mailie* turn'd her head,
An' clos'd her een amang the dead!

# Poor Mailie's Elegy

Lament in rhyme, lament in prose,
Wi' saut tears trickling down your nose;             salt
Our *Bardie's* fate is at a close,                   poet's
        Past a' remead!                              cure
The last, sad cape-stane of his woes;                coping-stone
    *Poor Mailie's* dead!

It's no the loss o' warl's gear,                  worldly property
That could sae bitter draw the tear,
Or make our *Bardie*, dowie, wear               sad
10          The mourning weed:
He's lost a friend and neebor dear,             neighbour
          In *Mailie* dead.

Thro' a' the town she trotted by him;           village/farm
A lang half-mile she could descry him;
Wi' kindly bleat, when she did spy him,
          She ran wi' speed:
A friend mair faithfu' ne'er came nigh him,
          Than *Mailie* dead.

I wat she was a *sheep* o' sense,               know
20   An' could behave hersel wi' mense:          discretion
I'll say't, she never brak a fence,             broke
          Thro' thievish greed.
Our *Bardie*, lanely, keeps the spence,         lonely, inner room
          Sin' *Mailie's* dead.

Or, if he wanders up the howe,                  valley
Her living image in *her yowe*,                 ewe
Comes bleating till him, owre the knowe,        to
          For bits o' bread;
An' down the briny pearls rowe                  roll
30          For *Mailie* dead.

She was nae get o' moorlan tips,                offspring, tups
Wi' tauted ket, an' hairy hips;                 matted fleece
For her forbears were brought in ships,
          Frae 'yont the TWEED:                  beyond
A bonier *fleesh* ne'er cross'd the clips       fleece, shears
          Than *Mailie's* dead.

Wae worth that man wha first did shape,         woe to
That vile, wanchancie thing – *a raep*!         unlucky, rope
It makes guid fellows girn an' gape,            'twist the features in
40          Wi' chokin dread;                    rage' (B)

An' *Robin's* bonnet wave wi' crape
    For *Mailie* dead.

O, a' ye *Bards* on bonie DOON!
An' wha on AIRE your chanters tune!
Come, join the melancholious croon       moan
    O' *Robin's* reed!
His heart will never get aboon!       above
    His *Mailie's* dead!


# To J. S****

*Friendship, mysterious cement of the soul!*
*Sweet'ner of Life, and solder of Society!*
*I owe thee much —*

          Blair


Dear S****, the sleest, pawkie thief,     cleverest, humorous
That e'er attempted stealth or rief,     plunder
Ye surely hae some warlock-breef     charm/wizard-spell
    Owre human hearts;
For ne'er a bosom yet was prief     proof
    Against your arts.

For me, I swear by sun an' moon,
And ev'ry star that blinks aboon,     above
Ye've cost me twenty pair o' shoon     shoes
10     Just gaun to see you;
And ev'ry ither pair that's done,
    Mair taen I'm wi' you.

That auld, capricious carlin, *Nature*,     old woman
To mak amends for scrimpet stature,     stunted
She's turn'd you off, a human-creature
    On her *first* plan,
And in her freaks, on ev'ry feature,
    She's wrote, *the Man.*

Just now I've taen the fit o' rhyme,
20 My barmie noddle's working prime,                yeasty brain
My fancy yerket up sublime                        stirred
     Wi' hasty summon:
Hae ye a leisure-moment's time
      To hear what's coming?

Some rhyme a neebor's name to lash;               neighbour
Some rhyme, (vain thought!) for needfu'
    cash;
Some rhyme to court the countra clash,            invite, talk
     An' raise a din;
For me, an *aim* I never fash;                    bother about
30      I rhyme for *fun*.

The star that rules my luckless lot,
Has fated me the russet coat,                     poor man's rural wear
An' damn'd my fortune to the groat;               small coin
     But, in requit,                   by way of
Has blest me with a *random-shot*                 compensation
     O' countra wit.

This while my notion's taen a sklent,             slant/turn
To try my fate in guid, black *prent*;            print
But still the mair I'm that way bent,
40      Something cries, 'hoolie!   'take leisure, stop!' (B)
I red you, honest man, tak tent!                  advise, take care
     Ye'll shaw your folly.            show

'There's ither Poets, much your betters,
Far seen in *Greek*, deep men o' *letters*,       well-versed
Hae thought they had ensur'd their debtors,       insured as
     A' future ages;
Now moths deform in shapeless tatters,
     Their unknown pages.'

Then farewell hopes of Laurel-boughs,
50 To garland my poetic brows!
Henceforth, I'll rove where busy ploughs
     Are whistling thrang,             busily

An' teach the lanely heights an' howes          lonely, hollows
        My rustic sang.

I'll wander on with tentless heed,              careless
How never-halting moments speed,
Till fate shall snap the brittle thread;
        Then, all unknown,
I'll lay me with th'*inglorious dead*,
60        Forgot and gone!

But why, o' Death, begin a tale?
Just now we're living sound an' hale;
Then top and maintop croud the sail,            crowd
        Heave *Care* o'er-side!
And large, before Enjoyment's gale,
        Let's tak the tide.

This life, sae far's I understand,              so far as
Is a' enchanted fairy-land,
Where Pleasure is the Magic-wand
70        That, wielded right,
Maks Hours like Minutes, hand in hand,
        Dance by fu' light.          full

The *magic-wand* then let us wield;
For, ance that five an' forty's speel'd,         climbed
See, crazy, weary, joyless Eild,                 Old Age
        Wi' wrinkl'd face,
Comes hostan, hirplan owre the field,            coughing, limping
        Wi' creeping pace.

When ance *life's day* draws near the gloamin,   twilight
80 Then fareweel vacant, careless roamin;
An' fareweel chearfu' tankards foamin,
        An' social noise;
An' fareweel dear, deluding woman,
        The joy of joys!

O *Life*! how pleasant in thy morning,
Young Fancy's rays the hills adorning!

Cold-pausing Caution's lessons scorning,
      We frisk away,
Like school-boys, at th' expected warning,
90        To joy and play.

We wander there, we wander here,
We eye the *rose* upon the brier,
Unmindful that the *thorn* is near,
      Among the leaves;
And tho' the puny wound appear,
      Short while it grieves.

Some, lucky, find a flow'ry spot,
For which they never toil'd nor swat;     sweated
They drink the *sweet* and eat the *fat*,
100      But care or pain;     without
And haply, eye the barren hut,
      With high disdain.

With steady aim, Some Fortune chase;
Keen hope does ev'ry sinew brace;
Thro' fair, thro' foul, they urge the race,
      And seize the prey:
Then canie, in some cozie place,     cautious, comfortable
      They close the *day*.

And others, like your humble servan',
110 *Poor wights*! nae rules nor roads observin;     fellows
To right or left, eternal swervin,
      They zig-zag on;
Till curst with Age, obscure an' starvin,
      They aften groan.

Alas! what bitter toil an' straining –
But truce with peevish, poor complaining!
Is Fortune's fickle *Luna* waning?     Moon
      E'en let her gang!
Beneath what light she has remaining,

120                    Let's sing our Sang.

My pen I here fling to the door,
And kneel, 'Ye *Pow'rs*', and warm implore,
'Tho' I should wander *Terra* o'er,                    Earth
          In all her climes,
Grant me but this, I ask no more,
          Ay rowth o' rhymes.                          plenty

'Gie dreeping roasts to *countra Lairds*,              dripping
Till icicles hing frae their beards;                   hang
Gie fine braw claes to fine *Life-guards*,             clothes
130          And *Maids of Honor*;
And yill an' whisky gie to *Cairds*,                   ale, tinkers
          Until they sconner.                          feel disgust

'A *Title*, DEMPSTER merits it;
A *Garter* gie to WILLIE PIT;
Gie Wealth to some be-ledger'd Cit,                    townsman
          In cent per cent;
But give me real, sterling Wit,
          And I'm content.

'While ye are pleas'd to keep me hale,                 healthy
140 I'll sit down o'er my scanty meal,
Be't *water-brose*, or *muslin-kail*,                  -porridge, meatless
          Wi' chearfu' face,                           broth
As lang's the Muses dinna fail
          To say the grace.'

An anxious e'e I never throws                          eye
Behint my lug, or by my nose;                          ear

I jouk beneath Misfortune's blows     *dodge*
    As weel's I may,
Sworn foe to *sorrow*, *care*, and *prose*,
150     I rhyme away.

O ye, douse folk, that live by rule,     *sedate*
Grave, tideless-blooded, calm and cool,
Compar'd wi' you – O fool! fool! fool!
    How much unlike!
Your hearts are just a standing pool,
    Your lives, a dyke!     *stone wall*

Nae hare-brain'd, sentimental traces,
In your unletter'd, nameless faces!
In *arioso* trills and graces
160     Ye never stray,
But *gravissimo*, solemn basses
    Ye hum away.

Ye are sae *grave*, nae doubt ye're *wise*;
Nae ferly tho' ye do despise     *wonder*
The hairum-scairum, ram-stam boys,     *wild, reckless*
    The rambling squad:
I see ye upward cast your eyes –
    – Ye ken the road –

Whilst I – but I shall haud me there –     *hold*
170 Wi' you I'll scarce gang *ony where* –
Then *Jamie*, I shall say nae mair,
    But quat my sang,     *end*
Content *with* YOU to mak a *pair*,
    Whare'er I gang.

# The Auld Farmer's New-Year-Morning Salutation to his Auld Mare, Maggie

## On Giving Her the Accustomed Ripp of Corn to Hansel in the New-Year

A *Guid New-Year* I wish you Maggie!
Hae, there's a ripp to thy auld baggie:      fist of unthreshed corn
                                                           belly
Tho' thou's howe-backet, now, an' knaggie,      'sunk in the back' (B)
         I've seen the day,                                 bony
Thou could hae gaen like ony staggie      colt
         Out owre the lay.                                 outfield

Tho' now thou's dowie, stiff an' crazy,      sickly, infirm
An' thy auld hide as white's a daisy,
I've seen thee dappl't, sleek an' glazie,      glittering smooth like
10          A bonie gray:                                 glass
He should been tight that daur't to *raize* thee,      capable, dared provoke
         Ance in a day.

Thou ance was i' the foremost rank,
A *filly* buirdly, steeve an' swank,      stately, strong, agile
An' set weel down a shapely shank,
         As e'er tread yird;                              earth
An' could hae flown out owre a stank,      pool of standing water
         Like onie bird.

It's now some nine-an'-twenty year,
20 Sin' thou was my *Guidfather's Meere*;      father-in-law's mare
He gied me thee, o' tocher clear,      dowry
         An' fifty mark;
Tho' it was sma', 'twas *weel-won* gear,      property
         An' thou was stark.                             strong

When first I gaed to woo my *Jenny*,
Ye then was trottan wi' your Minnie;          mother
Tho' ye was trickie, slee an' funnie,          clever
    Ye ne'er was donsie;          ill-tempered
But hamely, tawie, quiet an' cannie,          'that handles quietly' (B)
30     An' unco sonsie.          tractable

That *day*, ye pranc'd wi' muckle pride,
When ye bure hame my bonie *Bride*:          bore
An' sweet an' gracefu' she did ride
    Wi' maiden air!
KYLE-STEWART I could bragged wide,          have challenged
    For sic a *pair*.

Tho' now ye dow but hoyte and hoble,          can only move clumsily
An' wintle like a saumont-coble,          roll, salmon-boat
*That day*, ye was a jinker noble,          high-spirited beast
40     For heels an' win'!          wind
An' ran them till they a' did wauble          wobble
    Far, far behin'!

When thou an' I were young an' skiegh,          mettlesome
An' *Stable-meals* at Fairs were driegh,          dreary
How thou wad prance, an' snore, an' scriegh,          snort, neigh
    An' tak the road!
*Towns-bodies* ran, an' stood abiegh,          town folk, at a shy
    An' ca't thee mad.          distance

When thou was corn't, an' I was mellow,          fed with corn
50 We took the road ay like a Swallow:
At *Brooses* thou had ne'er a fellow,          wedding-races
    For pith an' speed;          energy
But ev'ry tail thou pay't them hollow,          beat
    Whare'er thou gaed.

The sma', droot-rumpl't, hunter cattle,          with drooping haunches, beasts
Might aiblins waur't thee for a brattle;          perhaps, beat, short race
But *sax Scotch mile*, thou try't their mettle,          six
    An' gart them whaizle:          made, wheeze
Nae whip nor spur, but just a wattle          stick
60     O' saugh or hazle.          willow

Thou was a noble *Fittie-lan'*,          rear left plough horse
As e'er in tug or tow was drawn!     leather or rope
Aft thee an' I, in aught hours gaun,    eight
      On guid March-weather,
Hae turn'd *sax rood* beside our han',  by ourselves
      For days thegither.

Thou never braing't, an' fetch't, an' flisket,  drew unsteadily, gasped, fretted
But thy *auld tail* thou wad hae whisket,
An' spread abreed thy weel-fill'd *brisket*,  abroad, breast
70      Wi' pith an pow'r,
Till sprittie knowes wad rair't an' risket  rushy, hillocks, roared, torn underfoot
      An' slypet owre.            fallen

When frosts lay lang, an' snaws were deep,  snows
An' threaten'd *labor* back to keep,
I gied thy *cog* a wee-bit heap        dish
      Aboon the timmer;       above, wooden edge
I ken'd my *Maggie* wad na sleep
      For that, or Simmer.     without, before summer

In *cart* or *car* thou never reestet;    stood restive
80  The steyest brae thou wad hae fac't it;  stiffest hill
Thou never lap, an' sten't, an' breastet,  leapt, reared, pulled forward
      Then stood to blaw;        blow
But just thy step a wee thing hastet,
      Thou snoov't awa.          went steadily on

My Pleugh is now thy *bairn-time* a';   plough-team, brood
Four gallant brutes, as e'er did draw;
Forby sax mae, I've sell't awa,      beside six more, sold
      That thou hast nurst:
They drew me thretteen pund an' twa,  thirteen
90      The vera warst.          worst

Monie a sair daurk we twa hae wrought,  hard day's labour
An' wi' the weary warl' fought!     world
An' monie an' *anxious day*, I thought
      We wad be beat!
Yet here to *crazy Age* we're brought,   infirm
      Wi' something yet.

An' think na, my auld, trusty *Servan*',
That now perhaps thou's less deservin,
An' thy *auld days* may end in starvin',    old age
      For my last fow,    firlot
A heapet *Stimpart*, I'll reserve ane    measure of grain/ quarter peck
      Laid by for you.

We've worn to crazy years thegither;    lived
We'll toyte about wi' ane anither;    totter/walk like old age
Wi' tentie care I'll flit thy tether,    watchful, change
      To some hain'd rig,    reserved field
Whare ye may nobly rax your leather,    stretch, skin
      Wi' sma' fatigue.

# The Cotter's Saturday Night

### Inscribed to R. A****, Esq

*Let not Ambition mock their useful toil,*
   *Their homely joys, and destiny obscure;*
*Nor Grandeur hear, with a disdainful smile,*
   *The short and simple annals of the Poor.*
                Gray

I

My lov'd, my honor'd, much respected
    friend,
   No mercenary Bard his homage pays;
With honest pride, I scorn each selfish end,
   My dearest meed, a friend's esteem and    reward
    praise:
To you I sing, in simple Scottish lays,
   The *lowly train* in life's sequester'd scene;
The native feelings strong, the guileless ways,
   What A**** in a *Cottage* would have
    been;

Ah! tho' his worth unknown, far happier
    there I ween!         *believe*

II

10 November chill blaws loud wi' angry sugh;  *blows, rushing sound*
    The short'ning winter-day is near a close;
The miry beasts retreating frae the pleugh;  *plough*
    The black'ning trains o' craws to their  *crows*
        repose:
The toil-worn COTTER frae his labor goes,  *farm tenant/cottager*
    *This night* his weekly moil is at an end,  *drudgery*
Collects his *spades*, his *mattocks* and his *hoes*,
    Hoping the *morn* in ease and rest to spend,
And weary, o'er the moor, his course does
        homeward bend.

III

At length his lonely *Cot* appears in view,  *cottage*
20     Beneath the shelter of an aged tree,
The expectant *wee-things*, toddlan, stacher  *stagger*
        through
    To meet their *Dad*, wi' flichterin noise  *fluttering*
        and glee,
His wee-bit ingle, blinkan bonilie,  *little bit of fire*
    His clean hearth-stane, his thrifty *Wifie's*  *stone*
        smile,
The *lisping infant*, prattling on his knee,
    Does a' his weary *kiaugh* and care beguile,  *'carking anxiety' (B)*
And makes him quite forget his labor and
        his toil.

IV

Belyve, the *elder bairns* come drapping in,  *soon, dropping*
    At *Service* out, amang the Farmers roun';
30 Some ca' the pleugh, some herd, some tentie  *drive, careful,*
       rin                             *run*
    A cannie errand to a neebor town:  *quiet, neighbouring*
Their eldest hope, their *Jenny*, woman-
        grown,

In youthfu' bloom, Love sparkling in her
    e'e,                                          *eye*
Comes hame, perhaps, to shew a braw new   *good-looking*
    gown,
  Or deposite her sair-won penny-fee,         *hard-won*
To help her *Parents* dear, if they in hardship
    be.

### V

With joy unfeign'd, *brothers* and *sisters* meet,
  And each for other's weelfare kindly spiers:  *asks*
The social hours, swift-wing'd, unnotic'd
    fleet;
40    Each tells the uncos that he sees or hears.  *news/uncommon*
The Parents partial eye their hopeful years;    *things*
  *Anticipation* forward points the view;
The *Mother*, wi' her needle and her sheers,
  Gars auld claes look amaist as weel's the  *makes, clothes*
    new;
The *Father* mixes a' wi' admonition due.

### VI

Their Master's and their Mistress's
    command,
  The *youngkers* a' are warned to obey;
And mind their labors wi' an eydent hand,   *diligent*
  And ne'er, tho' out of sight, to jauk or play:  'dally, trifle' (B)
50   'And O! be sure to fear the LORD alway!
  And mind your *duty*, duly, morn and night!
Lest in temptation's path ye gang astray,
  Implore his *counsel* and assisting *might*:
They nerve sought in vain that sought the
    LORD aright.'

### VII

But hark! a rap comes gently to the door;
  *Jenny*, wha kens the meaning o' the same,
Tells how a neebor lad came o'er the moor,
  To do some errands, and convoy her hame. *escort*
The wily Mother sees the *conscious flame*

60    Sparkle in *Jenny's* e'e, and flush her cheek,
    With heart-struck, anxious care enquires his
        name,
      While *Jenny* hafflins is afraid to speak;   half
    Weel-pleas'd the Mother hears, it's nae wild,
        worthless *Rake*.

### VIII

    With kindly welcome, *Jenny* brings him ben;
      A *strappan youth*; he takes the Mother's
        eye;
    Blythe *Jenny* sees the *visit's* no ill taen;
      The Father cracks of horses, pleughs and   talks
        kye.   cattle
    The *Youngster's* artless heart o'erflows wi'
        joy,
      But blate and laithfu', scarce can weel   shy, bashful
        behave;
70    The Mother, wi' a woman's wiles, can spy
      What makes the *youth* sae bashfu' and sae
        grave;
    Weel-pleas'd to think her *bairn's* respected
        like the lave.   rest

### IX

    O happy love! where love like this is found!
      O heart-felt raptures! bliss beyond
        compare!
    I've paced much this weary, *mortal round*,
      And sage EXPERIENCE bids me this
        declare –
    'If Heaven a draught of heavenly pleasure spare,
      One *cordial* in this melancholy *Vale*,
    'Tis when a youthful, loving, *modest* Pair,
80    In other's arms, breathe out the tender tale,
    Beneath the milk-white thorn that scents the
        ev'ning gale.'

### X

Is there, in human form, that bears a heart –
    A Wretch! a Villain! lost to love and truth!

That can, with studied, sly, ensnaring art,
    Betray sweet Jenny's unsuspecting youth?
Curse on his perjur'd arts! dissembling smooth!
    Are *Honor*, *Virtue*, *Conscience*, all exil'd?
Is there no Pity, no relenting Ruth,
    Points to the Parents fondling o'er their
        Child?
90 Then paints the *ruin'd Maid*, and *their*
    distraction wild!


XI

But now the Supper crowns their simple
    board,
    The healsome *Porritch*, chief of      wholesome, porridge
    SCOTIA's food:
The soupe their *only Hawkie* does afford,     drink, cow
    That 'yont the hallan snugly chows her     beyond, partition,
    cood:     chews, cud
The *Dame* brings forth, in complimental
    mood,
    To grace the lad, her weel-hain'd kebbuck, -kept, cheese
    fell,     pungent
And aft he's prest, and aft he ca's it guid;
    The frugal Wifie, garrulous, will tell,
How 'twas a towmond auld, sin' Lint was i'     twelvemonth, flax
    the bell.     flower


XII

100 The chearfu' Supper done, wi' serious face,
    They, round the ingle, form a circle wide;
The Sire turns o'er, with patriarchal grace,
    The big *ha'-Bible*, ance his *Father's* pride: hall-
His bonnet rev'rently is laid aside,
    His *lyart haffets* wearing thin and bare;     grey, temples
Those strains that once did sweet in ZION
    glide,
    He wales a portion with judicious care;     chooses
'*And let us worship GOD!*' he says with
    solemn air.

### XIII

They chant their artless notes in simple guise;
110     They tune their *hearts*, by far the noblest
            aim:
Perhaps *Dundee's* wild warbling measures
            rise,
     Or plaintive *Martyrs*, worthy of the name;
Or noble *Elgin* beets the heaven-ward flame,   'adds fuel to' (B)
     The sweetest far of SCOTIA's holy lays:
Compar'd with these, *Italian trills* are tame;
     The tickl'd ears no heart-felt raptures raise,
Nae unison hae they, with our CREATOR's
            praise.

### XIV

The priest-like Father reads the sacred page,
     How *Abram* was the Friend of GOD on
            high;
120 Or, *Moses* bade eternal warfare wage,
     With *Amalek's* ungracious progeny;
Or how the *royal Bard* did groaning lye,
     Beneath the stroke of Heaven's avenging
            ire;
Or *Job's* pathetic plaint, and wailing cry,
     Or rapt *Isaiah's* wild, seraphic fire;
Or other *Holy Seers* that tune the *sacred lyre*.

### XV

Perhaps the *Christian Volume* is the theme,
     How *guiltless blood* for *guilty man* was
            shed;
How HE, who bore in Heaven the second
            name,
130     Had not on Earth whereon to lay His head:
How His first *followers* and *servants* sped;
     The *Precepts sage* they wrote to many a
            land:
How *he*, who lone in *Patmos* banished,
     Saw in the sun a mighty angel stand;

And heard great *Bab'lon's* doom pronounc'd
    by Heaven's command.

#### XVI

Then kneeling down to HEAVEN's
    ETERNAL KING,
  The *Saint*, the *Father*, and the *Husband*
    prays:
Hope 'springs exulting on triumphant wing,'[1]
  That *thus* they all shall meet in future days:
140  There, ever bask in *uncreated rays*,
    No more to sigh, or shed the bitter tear,
*Together* hymning their CREATOR's praise,
  In *such society*, yet still more dear;
While circling Time moves round in an
    eternal sphere.

#### XVII

Compar'd with *this*, how poor Religion's
    pride,
  In all the pomp of *method*, and of *art*,
When men display to congregations wide,
  Devotion's ev'ry grace, except the *heart*!
The POWER, incens'd, the Pageant will
    desert,
150  The pompous strain, the sacerdotal stole;
But haply, in some *Cottage* far apart,
  May hear, well pleas'd, the language
    of the *Soul*;
And in His *Book of Life* the Inmates poor
    enroll.

#### XVIII

Then homeward all take off their sev'ral way;
  The youngling *Cottagers* retire to rest:
The Parent-pair their *secret homage* pay,
  And proffer up to Heaven the warm
    request,

---

[1] Pope's *Windsor Forest*.

That HE who stills the *raven's* clam'rous
    nest,
  And decks the *lily* fair in flow'ry pride,
160 Would, in the way *His Wisdom* sees the best,
  For *them* and for their *little ones* provide;
But chiefly, in their hearts with *Grace divine*
    preside.

#### XIX

From scenes like these, old SCOTIA's
    grandeur springs,
  That makes her lov'd at home, rever'd
    abroad:
Princes and lords are but the breath of kings,
  'An honest man's the noblest work of
    GOD:'
And *certes*, in fair Virtue's heavenly road,
  The *Cottage* leaves the *Palace* far behind:
What is a lordling's pomp? a cumbrous load,
170   Disguising oft the *wretch* of human kind,
Studied in arts of Hell, in wickedness refin'd!

#### XX

O SCOTIA! my dear, my native soil!
  For whom my warmest wish to Heaven is
    sent!
Long may thy hardy sons of *rustic toil*,
  Be blest with health, and peace, and sweet
    content!
And O may Heaven their simple lives prevent
  From *Luxury's* contagion, weak and vile!
Then howe'er *crowns* and *coronets* be rent,
  A *virtuous Populace* may rise the while,
180 And stand a wall of fire around their much-lov'd ISLE.

#### XXI

O THOU! who pour'd the *patriotic tide*,
  That stream'd thro' great, unhappy
    WALLACE' heart;

Who dar'd to, nobly, stem tyrannic pride,
   Or *nobly die*, the second glorious part:
(The Patriot's GOD, peculiarly thou art,
   His *friend*, *inspirer*, *guardian* and *reward*!)
O never, never SCOTIA's realm desert,
   But still the *Patriot*, and the *Patriot-Bard*,
In bright succession raise, her *Ornament*
         and *Guard*!


# To A Mouse

On turning her up in her Nest,
with the Plough, November, 1785


Wee, sleeket, cowran, tim'rous *beastie*,
   O, what a panic's in thy breastie!
Thou need na start awa sae hasty,
         Wi' bickering brattle!
I wad be laith to rin an' chase thee,
         Wi' murd'ring *pattle*!

I'm truly sorry Man's dominion
Has broken Nature's social union,
An' justifies that ill opinion,
         Which makes thee startle,
At me, thy poor, earth-born companion,
         An' *fellow-mortal*!

I doubt na, whyles, but thou may *thieve*;
What then? poor beastie, thou maun live!
A *daimen-icker* in a *thrave*
         'S a sma' request:
I'll get a blessin wi' the lave,
         An' never miss't!

*(glosses)*
sleek, fearful, little creature
little breast
sound of scamper
loath, run
plough-staff
occasional ear, 24 sheaves
what's left/the rest

10

Thy wee-bit *housie*, too, in ruin!
20  Its silly wa's the win's are strewin!                          frail, winds
An' naething, now, to big a new ane,                          build
   O' foggage green!                                rank grass
An' bleak *December's winds* ensuin,
   Baith snell an' keen!                             bitter

Thou saw the fields laid bare an' wast,                       waste
An' weary *Winter* comin fast,
An' cozie here, beneath the blast,
   Thou thought to dwell,
Till crash! the cruel *coulter* past                          iron cutter of plough
30     Out thro' thy cell.

That wee-bit heap o' leaves an' stibble,                      stubble
Has cost thee monie a weary nibble!
Now thou's turn'd out, for a' thy trouble,
   But house or hald,                             without refuge
To thole the Winter's *sleety dribble*,                       endure
   An' *cranreuch* cauld!                         hoar-frost

But Mousie, thou art no thy-lane,                             not alone
In proving *foresight* may be vain:
The best laid schemes o' *Mice* an' *Men*,
40     Gang aft agley,                            awry
An' lea'e us nought but grief an' pain,
   For promis'd joy!

Still, thou art blest, compar'd wi' *me*!
The *present* only toucheth thee:
But Och! I *backward* cast my e'e,                            eye
   On prospects drear!
An' *forward*, tho' I canna *see*,
   I *guess* an' *fear*!

# To A Mountain-Daisy

On turning one down, with the Plough,
in April —— 1786


Wee, modest, crimson-tipped flow'r,
Thou's met me in an evil hour;
For I maun crush amang the stoure          dust
        Thy slender stem:
To spare thee now is past my pow'r,
        Thou bonie gem.

Alas! it's no thy neebor sweet,            neighbour
The bonie *Lark*, companion meet!
Bending thee 'mang the dewy weet!          wet
10        Wi's spreckl'd breast,
When upward-springing, blythe, to greet
        The purpling East.

Cauld blew the bitter-biting *North*
Upon thy early, humble birth;
Yet chearfully thou glinted forth
        Amid the storm,
Scarce rear'd above the *Parent-earth*
        Thy tender form.

The flaunting *flow'rs* our Gardens yield,
20 High-shelt'ring woods and wa's maun shield,
But thou, beneath the random bield         shelter
        O' clod or stane,                  stone
Adorns the histie *stibble-field*,         bare, stubble-
        Unseen, alane.                     alone

There, in thy scanty mantle clad,
Thy snawie bosom sun-ward spread,          snowy

Thou lifts thy unassuming head
          In humble guise;
But now the *share* uptears thy bed,          ploughshare
30          And low thou lies!

Such is the fate of artless Maid,
Sweet *flow'ret* of the rural shade!
By Love's simplicity betray'd,
          And guileless trust,
Till she, like thee, all soil'd, is laid
          Low i' the dust.

Such is the fate of simple Bard,
On Life's rough ocean luckless starr'd!
Unskilful he to note the card
40          Of *prudent Lore*,
Till billows rage, and gales blow hard,
          And whelm him o'er!

Such fate to *suffering worth* is giv'n,
Who long with wants and woes has striv'n,
By human pride or cunning driv'n
          To Mis'ry's brink,
Till wrench'd of ev'ry stay but HEAV'N,
          He, ruin'd, sink!

Ev'n thou who mourn'st the *Daisy's* fate,
50 *That fate is thine* – no distant date;
Stern Ruin's *plough-share* drives, elate,
          Full on thy bloom,
Till crush'd beneath the *furrow's* weight,
          Shall be thy doom!

# Epistle
# To A Young Friend

### May —— 1786

#### I

I Lang hae thought, my youthfu' friend,
    A Something to have sent you,
Tho' it should serve nae other end
    Than just a kind memento;
But how the subject theme may gang,
    Let time and chance determine,
Perhaps it may turn out a Sang;
    Perhaps, turn out a Sermon.

#### II

Ye'll try the world soon my lad,
    And ANDREW dear believe me,
Ye'll find mankind an unco squad,
    And muckle they may grieve ye:
For care and trouble set your thought,
    Ev'n when your end's attained;
And a' your views may come to nought,
    Where ev'ry nerve is strained.

#### III

I'll no say, men are villains a';
    The real, harden'd wicked,
Whae hae nae check but *human law*,
    Are to a few restricked:
But Och, mankind are unco weak,
    An' little to be trusted;
If *Self* the wavering balance shake,
    It's rarely right adjusted!

#### IV

Yet they wha fa' in Fortune's strife,
    Their fate we should na censure,
For still th'*important end* of life,

They equally may answer:
A man may hae an *honest heart*,
30    Tho' Poortith hourly stare him;                    poverty
A man may tak a neebor's part,                          neighbour's
Yet hae nae *cash* to spare him.


V

Ay free, aff han', your story tell,                     offhand
When wi' a bosom crony;
But still keep something to yoursel
Ye scarcely tell to ony.
Conceal yoursel as weel's ye can
Frae critical dissection;
But keek thro' ev'ry other man,                         look/pry
40    Wi' sharpen'd, sly inspection.


VI

The *sacred lowe* o' weel plac'd love,                  flame
Luxuriantly indulge it;
But never tempt th'*illicit rove*,                      attempt
Tho' naething should divulge it:
I waive the quantum o' the sin;                         amount
The hazard of concealing;
But Och! it hardens *a' within*,
And petrifies the feeling!


VII

To catch Dame Fortune's golden smile,
50    Assiduous wait upon her;
And gather gear by ev'ry wile,                          money/property
That's justify'd by Honor:
Not for to *hide* it in a *hedge*,
Nor for a *train-attendant*;
But for the glorious priviledge
Of being *independant*.


VIII

*The fear o' Hell's* a hangman's whip,
To haud the wretch in order;                            hold
But where ye feel your *Honor* grip,

60      Let that ay be your border:
Its slightest touches, instant pause –
    Debar a' side-pretences;
And resolutely keep its laws,
    Uncaring consequences.

### IX

The great CREATOR to revere,
    Must sure become the *Creature*;
But still the preaching cant forbear,
    And ev'n the rigid feature:
Yet ne'er with Wits prophane to range,
70      Be complaisance extended;
An *atheist-laugh's* a poor exchange
    For *Deity offended*!

### X

When ranting round in Pleasure's ring,        frolicking
    Religion may be blinded;
Or if she gie a *random-fling*,
    It may be little minded;
But when on Life we're tempest-driven,
    A Conscience but a canker –
A correspondence fix'd wi' Heav'n,
80      Is sure a noble *anchor*!

### XI

Adieu, dear, amiable Youth!
    Your *heart* can ne'er be wanting!
May Prudence, Fortitude and Truth
    Erect your brow undaunting!
In *ploughman phrase* 'GOD send you speed,'
    Still daily to grow wiser;
And may ye better reck the *rede*,        heed the advice
    Than ever did th'*Adviser*!

# On a Scotch Bard
# gone to the West Indies

A' ye wha live by sowps o' drink,      *mouthfuls*
A' ye wha live by crambo-clink,      *rhyme*
A' ye wha live and never think,
        Come, mourn wi' me!
Our *billie's* gien us a' a jink,      *comrade, slip*
        An' owre the Sea.

Lament him a' ye rantan core,      *merry company*
Wha dearly like a random-splore;      *frolic*
Nae mair he'll join the *merry roar*,
10         In social key;
For now he's taen anither shore,
        An' owre the Sea!

The bonie lasses weel may wiss him,      *wish*
And in their dear *petitions* place him:
The widows, wives, an' a' may bless him,
        Wi' tearfu' e'e;      *eye*
For weel I wat they'll sairly miss him      *know*
        That's owre the Sea!

O Fortune, they hae room to grumble!
20 Hadst thou taen aff some drowsy bummle,      *bungler*
Wha can do nought but fyke an' fumble,      *fuss*
        'Twad been nae plea;
But he was gleg as onie wumble,      *nimble, gimlet*
        That's owre the Sea!

Auld, cantie KYLE may weepers wear,      *cheerful*
An' stain them wi' the saut, saut tear:      *salt*
'Twill mak her poor, auld heart, I fear,
        In flinders flee:      *fragments*
He was her *Laureat* monie a year,
30         That's owre the Sea!

He saw Misfortune's cauld *Nor-west*
Lang-mustering up a bitter blast;
A Jillet brak his heart at last,    jilt
    Ill may she be!
So, took a birth afore the mast,    berth
    An' owre the Sea,

To tremble under Fortune's cummock;    cudgel
On scarce a bellyfu' o' *drummock*,    meal and water
Wi' his proud, independant stomach,
40    Could ill agree;
So, row't his hurdies in a *hammock*,    rolled, buttocks
    An' owre the Sea.

He ne'er was gien to great misguidin,
Yet coin his pouches wad na bide in;    pockets
Wi' him it ne'er was *under hidin*;
    He dealt it free:
The *Muse* was a' that he took pride in,
    That's owre the Sea.

*Jamaica bodies*, use him weel,
50 An' hap him in a cozie biel:    wrap, shelter
Ye'll find him ay a dainty chiel,    pleasant fellow
    An' fou o' glee:    full
He wad na wrang'd the vera *Diel*,    wronged, very, Devil
    That's owre the Sea.

Fareweel, my *rhyme-composing billie*!    fellow
Your native soil was right ill-willie;    unkind
But may ye flourish like a lily,
    Now bonilie!
I'll toast you in my hindmost *gillie*,    last gill
60    Tho' owre the Sea!

# To A Louse

## On Seeing one on a Lady's Bonnet at Church

Ha! whare ye gaun, ye crowlan ferlie!      *crawling wonder*
Your impudence protects you sairly:      *indeed*
I canna say but ye strunt rarely,      *strut*
       Owre *gawze* and *lace*;
Tho' faith, I fear ye dine but sparely,
       On sic a place.

Ye ugly, creepan, blastet wonner,      *wonder*
Detested, shunn'd, by saunt an' sinner,      *saint*
How daur ye set your fit upon her,      *dare, foot*
10        Sae fine a *Lady*!
Gae somewhere else and seek your dinner,
       On some poor body.

Swith, in some beggar's haffet squattle;      *off!, temple, squat*
There ye may creep, and sprawl, and sprattle,      *scramble*
Wi' ither kindred, jumping cattle,      *beasts*
       In shoals and nations;      *families, tribes*
Whare *horn* nor *bane* ne'er daur unsettle,      *horn, bone*
       Your thick plantations.

Now haud you there, ye're out of sight,      *keep*
20 Below the fatt'rels, snug and tight,      *falderals*
Na faith ye yet! ye'll no be right,
       Till ye've got on it,
The vera tapmost, towrin height      *very topmost*
       O' *Miss's bonnet*.

My sooth! right bauld ye set your nose out,      *bold*
As plump an' gray as onie grozet:      *gooseberry*
O for some rank, mercurial rozet,      *resin*
       Or fell, red smeddum,      *deadly, powder*
I'd gie you sic a hearty dose o't,
30        Wad dress your droddum!      *thrash, backside*

I wad na been surpriz'd to spy
You on an auld wife's *flainen toy*;                    flannel cap
Or aiblins some bit duddie boy,                         perhaps, small ragged
     On's *wylecoat*;                            flannel vest
But Miss's fine *Lunardi*, fye!                         balloon bonnet
     How daur ye do't?

O *Jenny* dinna toss your head,                         do not
An' set your beauties a' abread!                        abroad
Ye little ken what cursed speed
40      The blastie's makin!                   ill-disposed creature
Thae *winks* and *finger-ends*, I dread,                those
     Are notice takin!

O wad some Pow'r the giftie gie us                      little gift
*To see oursels as others see us*!
It wad frae monie a blunder free us
     An' foolish notion:
What airs in dress an' gait wad lea'e us
     And ev'n Devotion!

# Epistle to J. L*****k

## An Old Scotch Bard

### April 1st, 1785

While briers an' woodbines budding green,
An' Paitricks scraichan loud at e'en,                   partridges, screaming, evening
And morning Poossie whiddan seen,                       hare, scudding
     Inspire my Muse,
This freedom, in an *unknown* frien',
     I pray excuse.

On Fasteneen we had a rockin,                           Shrove Tuesday, spinning party
To ca' the crack and weave our stockin;                have a chat

And there was muckle fun and jokin,
  Ye need na doubt;
At length we had a hearty yokin,   set-to
  At *sang about*.   singing in turn

There was ae *sang*, amang the rest,
Aboon them a' it pleas'd me best,   above
That some kind husband had addrest,
  To some sweet wife:
It thirl'd the heart-strings thro' the breast,   thrilled
  A' to the life.

I've scarce heard ought describ'd sae weel,
What gen'rous, manly bosoms feel;
Thought I, 'Can this be *Pope*, or *Steele*,
  Or *Beattie's* wark;'   work
They tale me 'twas an odd kind chiel   told, fellow
  About *Muirkirk*.

It pat me fidgean-fain to hear't,   put, tingling with pleasure
An' sae about him there I spier't;   asked
Then a' that kent him round declar'd,
  He had *ingine*,   wit
That name excell'd it, few cam near't,
  It was sae fine.

That set him to a pint of ale,
An' either douse or merry tale,   sober
Or rhymes an' sangs he'd made himsel,
  Or witty catches,
'Tween Inverness and Teviotdale,
  He had few matches.

Then up I gat, an swoor an aith,   swore, oath
Tho' I should pawn my pleugh an' graith,   plough, harness
Or die a cadger pownie's death,   hawker pony's
  At some dyke-back,   behind a wall
A *pint* an' *gill* I'd gie them *baith*,
  To hear your crack.   talk

But first an' foremost, I should tell,
Amaist as soon as I could spell,
I to the *crambo-jingle* fell,       rhyming
     Tho' rude an' rough,
Yet crooning to a body's sel,       humming, to oneself
     Does weel eneugh.       enough

50  I am nae *Poet*, in a sense,
But just a *Rhymer* like by chance,
An' hae to Learning nae pretence,
     Yet, what the matter?
Whene'er my Muse does on me glance,
     I jingle at her.

Your Critic-folk may cock their nose,
And say, 'How can you e'er propose,
You wha ken hardly *verse* frae *prose*,
     To mak a *sang*?'
But by your leaves, my learned foes,
60       Ye're maybe wrang.       wrong

What's a' your jargon o' your Schools,
Your Latin names for horns an' stools;
If honest Nature made you *fools*,
     What sairs your Grammars?       serves
Ye'd better taen up *spades* and *shools*,       shovels
     Or *knappin-hammers*.       stone-breaking

A set o' dull, conceited Hashes,
Confuse their brains in *Colledge-classes*!
They *gang* in Stirks, and *come out* Asses,       steers/young bullocks
70       Plain truth to speak;
An' syne they think to climb Parnassus       then
     By dint o' Greek!

Gie me ae spark o' Nature's fire,
That's a' the learning I desire;
Then tho' I drudge thro' dub an' mire       puddle
     At pleugh or cart,
My Muse, tho' hamely in attire,

May touch the heart.

O for a spunk o' ALLAN's glee,                    spark
80 Or FERGUSSON's, the bauld an' slee,             bold, clever
Or bright L*****K's, my friend to be,
        If I can hit it!
That would be *lear* enuegh for me,               learning
        If I could get it.

Now, Sir, if ye hae friends enow,                 enough
Tho' *real friends* I b'lieve are few,
Yet, if your catalogue be fow,                    full
        I'se no insist;                           I'll
But gif ye want ae friend that's true,            if
90        I'm on your list.

I winna blaw about *mysel*,                        will not brag
As ill I like my fauts to tell;                   faults
But friends an' folk that wish me well,
        They sometimes roose me;                  praise
Tho' I maun own, as monie still,
        As far abuse me.

There's ae *wee faut* they whiles lay to me,
I like the lasses – Gude forgie me!               God forgive
For monie a Plack they wheedle frae me,           coin
100        At dance or fair:
Maybe some *ither thing* they gie me
        They weel can spare.

But MAUCHLINE Race or MAUCHLINE Fair,
I should be proud to meet you there;
We'se gie ae night's discharge to *care*,         we'll
        If we forgather,
An' hae a swap o' *rhymin-ware*,
        Wi' ane anither.

The *four-gill chap*, we'se gar him clatter,       cup, we'll make
110 An' kirs'n him wi' reekin water;              christen, steaming
Syne we'll sit down an' tak our whitter,          draught

To chear our heart;
An' faith, we'se be *acquainted* better
    Before we part.

Awa ye selfish, warly race,                              worldly
Wha think that havins, sense an' grace,                  manners
Ev'n love an' friendship should give place
    To *catch-the-plack*!                coining money
I dinna like to see your face,                           do not
120     Nor hear your crack.

But ye whom social pleasure charms,
Whose hearts the *tide of kindness* warms,
Who hold your *being* on the terms,
    'Each aids the others,'
Come to my bowl, come to my arms,
    My friends, my brothers!

But to conclude my lang epistle,
As my auld pen's worn to the grissle;
Twa lines frae you wad gar me fissle,                    make, tingle
130     Who am, most fervent,
While I can either sing, or whissle,
    Your friend and servant.

# Song

### Tune, Corn rigs are bonie

### I

It was upon a Lammas night,
    When corn rigs are bonie,                ridges
Beneath the moon's unclouded light,
    I held awa to Annie:                     took my way
The time flew by, wi' tentless heed,                     careless
    Till 'tween the late and early;

Wi' sma' persuasion she agreed,
  To see me thro' the barley.


## II

    The sky was blue, the wind was still,
10    The moon was shining clearly;
I set her down, wi' right good will,
  Amang the rigs o' barley:
I ken't her heart was a' my ain;        *own*
  I lov'd her most sincerely;
I kiss'd her owre and owre again,
  Amang the rigs o' barley.


## III

I lock'd her in my fond embrace;
  Her heart was beating rarely:
My blessings on that happy place,
20    Amang the rigs o' barley!
But by the moon and stars so bright,
  That shone that night so clearly!
She ay shall bless that happy night,
  Amang the rigs o' barley.


## IV

I hae been blythe wi' Comrades dear;
  I hae been merry drinking;
I hae been joyfu' gath'rin gear;       *money/property*
  I hae been happy thinking;
But a' the pleasures e'er I saw,
30    Tho' three times doubl'd fairly,
That happy night was worth them a',
  Amang the rigs o' barley.


### CHORUS

Corn rigs, an' barley rigs,
  An' corn rigs are bonie:
I'll ne'er forget that happy night,
  Amang the rigs wi' Annie.

# Song

## Composed in August
### Tune, I had a horse, I had nae mair

I

Now westlin winds, and slaught'ring guns     westerly
  Bring Autumn's pleasant weather;
And the moorcock springs, on whirring
    wings,
  Amang the blooming heather:
Now waving grain, wide o'er the plain,
  Delights the weary Farmer;
And the moon shines bright, when I rove at
    night,
  To muse upon my Charmer.

II

The Partridge loves the fruitful fells;
10    The Plover loves the mountains;
The Woodcock haunts the lonely dells;
  The soaring Hern the fountains:
Thro' lofty groves, the Cushat roves,     wood-pigeon
  The path of man to shun it;
The hazel bush o'erhangs the Thrush,
  The spreading thorn the Linnet.

III

Thus ev'ry kind their pleasure find,
  The savage and the tender;
Some social join, and leagues combine;
20    Some solitary wander:
Avaunt, away! the cruel sway,
  Tyrannic man's dominion;
The Sportsman's joy, the murd'ring cry,
  The flutt'ring, gory pinion!

### IV

But PEGGY dear, the ev'ning's clear,
    Thick flies the skimming Swallow;
The sky is blue, the fields in view,
    All fading-green and yellow:
Come let us stray our gladsome way,
30    And view the charms of Nature;
The rustling corn, the fruited thorn,
    And ev'ry happy creature.

### V

We'll gently walk, and sweetly talk,
    Till the silent moon shine clearly;
I'll grasp thy waist, and fondly prest,
    Swear how I love thee dearly:
Not vernal show'rs to budding flow'rs,
    Not Autumn to the Farmer,
So dear can be, as thou to me,
40    My fair, my lovely Charmer!

# A Bard's Epitaph

Is there a whim-inspir'd fool,
Owre fast for thought, owre hot for rule,    too
Owre blate to seek, owre proud to snool,    diffident, submit tamely
    Let him draw near;
And o'er this grassy heap sing dool,    lament
    And drap a tear.    drop

Is there a Bard of rustic song,
Who, noteless, steals the crouds among,
That weekly this area throng,    churchyard
10    O, pass not by!
But with a frater-feeling strong,    brother
    Here, heave a sigh.

Is there a man whose judgment clear,

Can others teach the course to steer,
Yet runs, himself, life's mad career,
      Wild as the wave,
Here pause – and thro' the starting tear,
      Survey this grave.

The poor Inhabitant below
20 Was quick to learn and wise to know,
And keenly felt the friendly glow,
      And *softer flame*;
But thoughtless follies laid him low,
      And stain'd his name!

Reader attend – whether thy soul
Soars fancy's flights beyond the pole,
Or darkling grubs this earthly hole,
      In low pursuit,
Know, prudent, cautious, *self-controul*
30       Is Wisdom's root.

# Holy Willie's Prayer

*And send the Godly in a pet to pray –*
                   Pope

ARGUMENT

Holy Willie was a rather oldish batchelor Elder in the
parish of Mauchline, and much and justly famed for that
polemical chattering which ends in tippling Orthodoxy,
and for that Spiritualized Bawdry which refines to
Liquorish Devotion. – In a Sessional process with a
gentleman in Mauchline, a Mr Gavin Hamilton, Holy
Willie, and his priest, father Auld, after full hearing in the
Presbytery of Ayr, came off but second best; owing partly
to the oratorical powers of Mr Robt Aiken, Mr Hamilton's
Counsel; but chiefly to Mr Hamilton's being one of the
most irreproachable and truly respectable characters in

the country. – On losing his Process, the Muse overheard
him at his devotions as follows –

O Thou that in the heavens does dwell!
Wha, as it pleases best thysel,
Sends ane to heaven and ten to h-ll,
          A' for thy glory!
And no for ony gude or ill
          They've done before thee. –

I bless and praise thy matchless might,
When thousands thou has left in night,
That I am here before thy sight,
10          For gifts and grace,
A burning and a shining light
          To a' this place. –

What was I, or my generation,
That I should get such exaltation?
I, wha deserv'd most just damnation,
          For broken laws
Sax thousand years ere my creation,
          Thro' Adam's cause!

When from my mother's womb I fell,
20  Thou might hae plunged me deep in hell,
To gnash my gooms, and weep, and wail,        gums
          In burning lakes,
Where damned devils roar and yell
          Chain'd to their stakes. –

Yet I am here, a chosen sample,
To shew thy grace is great and ample:
I'm here, a pillar o' thy temple
          Strong as a rock,
A guide, a ruler and example
30          To a' thy flock. –

[O L—d thou kens what zeal I bear,
When drinkers drink, and swearers swear,

And singin' there, and dancin' here,
　　　Wi' great an' sma';
For I am keepet by thy fear,
　　　Free frae them a'. –]


But yet – O L—d – confess I must –
At times I'm fash'd wi' fleshly lust;                    afflicted
And sometimes too, in warldly trust
40　　　Vile Self gets in;
But thou remembers we are dust,
　　　Defil'd wi' sin. –


O L—d – yestreen – thou kens – wi' Meg –
Thy pardon I sincerely beg!
O may't ne'er be a living plague,
　　　To my dishonor!
And I'll ne'er lift a lawless leg
　　　Again upon her. –


Besides, I farther maun avow,                           must
50 Wi' Leezie's lass, three times – I trow –
But L—d, that friday I was fou                          drunk
　　　When I cam near her;
Or else, thou kens, thy servant true
　　　Wad never steer her. –


Maybe thou lets this fleshly thorn
Buffet thy servant e'en and morn,
Lest he o'er proud and high should turn,
　　　That he's sae gifted;
If sae, thy hand maun e'en be borne
60　　　Untill thou lift it. –


L—d bless thy Chosen in this place,
For here thou has a chosen race:
But G-d, confound their stubborn face,
　　　And blast their name,
Wha bring thy rulers to disgrace
　　　And open shame. –

L—d mind Gaun Hamilton's deserts!
He drinks, and swears, and plays at cartes,    cards
Yet has sae mony taking arts
      Wi' Great and Sma',
70
Frae G-d's ain priest the people's hearts
      He steals awa. –

And when we chasten'd him therefore,
Thou kens how he bred sic a splore,    uproar
And set the warld in a roar
      O' laughin at us:
Curse thou his basket and his store,
      Kail and potatoes. –    cabbage

L—d hear my earnest cry and prayer
80  Against that Presbytry of Ayr!
Thy strong right hand, L—d, make it bare
      Upon their heads!
L—d visit them, and dinna spare,
      For their misdeeds!

O L—d my G-d, that glib-tongu'd Aiken!
My very heart and flesh are quaking
To think how I sat, sweating, shaking,
      And p-ss'd wi' dread,
While Auld wi' hingin lip gaed sneaking
90        And hid his head!

L—d, in thy day o' vengeance try him!
L—d visit him that did employ him!
And pass not in thy mercy by them,
      Nor hear their prayer;
But for thy people's sake destroy them,
      And dinna spare!

But L—d, remember me and mine
Wi' mercies temporal and divine!
That I for grace and gear may shine,
100        Excell'd by nane!

And a' the glory shall be thine!
   AMEN! AMEN!


# Tam o' Shanter. A Tale

*Of Brownyis and of Bogillis full is this buke.*
           Gawin Douglas


| | |
|---|---|
| When chapman billies leave the street, | pedlar lads |
| And drouthy neebors, neebors meet, | thirsty neighbours |
| As market-days are wearing late, | |
| An' folk begin to tak the gate; | take the road |
| While we sit bousing at the nappy, | boozing, ale |
| And getting fou and unco happy, | drunk |
| We think na on the lang Scots miles, | |
| The mosses, waters, slaps, and styles, | gaps in walls |
| That lie between us and our hame, | |
| Whare sits our sulky sullen dame, | |
| Gathering her brows like gathering storm, | |
| Nursing her wrath to keep it warm. | |

10

| | |
|---|---|
| This truth fand honest *Tam o' Shanter*, | found |
| As he frae Ayr ae night did canter, | |
| (Auld Ayr, wham ne'er a town surpasses, | old |
| For honest men and bonny lasses.) | |

| | |
|---|---|
| O *Tam*! hadst thou but been sae wise, | |
| As ta'en thy ain wife *Kate's* advice! | own |
| She tauld thee weel thou was a skellum, | told, well, rascal |
| A blethering, blustering, drunken blellum; | babbler |
| That frae November till October, | |
| Ae market-day thou was nae sober; | |
| That ilka melder, wi' the miller, | time for corn-grinding |
| Thou sat as lang as thou had siller; | silver |
| That every naig was ca'd a shoe on; | [time a] pony was shod |
| The smith and thee gat roaring fou on; | |
| That at the L—d's house, even on Sunday, | |

20

Thou drank wi' Kirkton Jean till Monday.
She prophesied that late or soon,
30   Thou would be found deep drown'd in Doon;
Or catch'd wi' warlocks in the mirk,          caught, darkness
By *Alloway's* auld haunted kirk.

    Ah, gentle dames! it gars me greet,          makes, weep
To think how mony counsels sweet,
How mony lengthen'd sage advices,
The husband frae the wife despises!

    But to our tale: Ae market-night,
*Tam* had got planted unco right;          just
Fast by an ingle, bleezing finely,          fireside, blazing
40   Wi' reaming swats, that drank divinely;          foaming beer
And at his elbow, Souter *Johnny*,          Shoemaker
His ancient, trusty, drouthy crony;
*Tam* lo'ed him like a vera brither;          loved, real brother
They had been fou for weeks thegither.          together
The night drave on wi' sangs and clatter;          drove, gossip
And ay the ale was growing better:
The landlady and *Tam* grew gracious,
Wi' favours, secret, sweet, and precious:
The Souter tauld his queerest stories;          told
50   The landlord's laugh was ready chorus:
The storm without might rair and rustle,          roar
*Tam* did na mind the storm a whistle.

    Care, mad to see a man sae happy,
E'en drown'd himsel amang the nappy:          even
As bees flee hame wi' lades o' treasure,          fly, loads
The minutes wing'd their way wi' pleasure:
Kings may be blest, but *Tam* was glorious,
O'er a' the ills o' life victorious!

    But pleasures are like poppies spread,
60   You seize the flower, its bloom is shed;
Or like the snow falls in the river,
A moment white – then melts for ever;
Or like the borealis race,

That flit ere you can point their place;
Or like the rainbow's lovely form
Evanishing amid the storm. –
Nae man can tether time or tide;
The hour approaches *Tam* maun ride;
That hour, o' night's black arch the
      key-stane,          -stone
70 That dreary hour he mounts his beast in;
And sic a night he taks the road in,
As ne'er poor sinner was abroad in.

The wind blew as 'twad blawn its last;    if blowing
The rattling showers rose on the blast;
The speedy gleams the darkness swallow'd;
Loud, deep, and lang, the thunder bellow'd:
That night, a child might understand,
The Deil had business on his hand.    Devil

Weel mounted on his gray mare, *Meg*,
80 A better never lifted leg,
*Tam* skelpit on thro' dub and mire,    hurried, mud
Despising wind, and rain, and fire;
Whiles holding fast his gude blue bonnet;
Whiles crooning o'er some auld Scots sonnet;
Whiles glowring round wi' prudent cares,
Lest bogles catch him unawares:    spectres/goblins
*Kirk-Alloway* was drawing nigh,
Whare ghaists and houlets nightly cry. –    ghosts, owls

By this time he was cross the ford,
90 Whare, in the snaw, the chapman smoor'd;    snow, smothered
And past the birks and meikle stane,    birches, stone
Whare drunken *Charlie* brak's neck-bane;    broke, -bone
And thro' the whins, and by the cairn,
Whare hunters fand the murder'd bairn;    child
And near the thorn, aboon the well,    above
Whare *Mungo's* mither hang'd hersel. –    mother
Before him *Doon* pours all his floods;
The doubling storm roars thro' the woods;
The lightnings flash from pole to pole;

100  Near and more near the thunders roll:
     When, glimmering thro' the groaning trees,
     *Kirk-Alloway* seem'd in a bleeze;
     Thro' ilka bore the beams were glancing;          crevice
     And loud resounded mirth and dancing. –

          Inspiring bold *John Barleycorn*!
     What dangers thou canst make us scorn!
     Wi' tippeny, we fear nae evil;                    ale at 2d a pint
     Wi' usquabae, we'll face the devil! –             whisky
     The swats sae ream'd in *Tammie's* noddle,        head
110  Fair play, he car'd na deils a boddle.            worthless coin
     But *Maggie* stood right sair astonish'd,         sore
     Till, by the heel and hand admonish'd,
     She ventured forward on the light;
     And, vow! *Tam* saw an unco sight!
     Warlocks and witches in a dance;
     Nae cotillion brent new frae France,             brand
     But hornpipes, jigs, strathspeys, and reels,
     Put life and mettle in their heels.
     A winnock-bunker in the east,                     window-seat
120  There sat auld Nick, in shape o' beast;          The Devil
     A towzie tyke, black, grim, and large,           ragged mongrel
     To gie them music was his charge:                give
     He screw'd the pipes, and gart them skirl,       made shriek
     Till roof and rafters a' did dirl. –             shake
     Coffins stood round, like open presses,          cupboards
     That shaw'd the dead in their last dresses;      showed
     And by some devilish cantraip slight             magic/trick
     Each in its cauld hand held a light. –           cold
     By which heroic *Tam* was able
130  To note upon the haly table,                     holy
     A murderer's banes in gibbet-airns;              bones, -irons
     Twa span-lang, wee, unchristen'd bairns;         nine-inch, small
     A thief, new-cutted frae a rape,                 rope
     Wi' his last gasp his gab did gape;              mouth
     Five tomahawks, wi' blude red-rusted;            blood
     Five scimitars, wi' murder crusted;
     A garter, which a babe had strangled;
     A knife, a father's throat had mangled,

Whom his ain son o' life bereft,
140 The grey hairs yet stack to the heft;          stuck
Wi' mair o' horrible and awefu',
Which even to name wad be unlawfu'.

   As *Tammie* glowr'd, amazed, and curious,
The mirth and fun grew fast and furious:
The piper loud and louder blew
The dancers quick and quicker flew;
They reel'd, they set, they cross'd, they          linked arms
      cleekit,
Till ilka carlin swat and reekit,          witch, sweated, reeked
And coost her duddies to the wark,          cast, rags, work
150 And linket at it in her sark!          shift

   Now, *Tam*, O *Tam*! had thae been queans,          young girls
A' plump and strapping in their teens,
Their sarks, instead o' creeshie flannen,          greasy flannel
Been snaw-white seventeen hunder linnen!          best linen
Thir breeks o' mine, my only pair,          these trousers
That ance were plush, o' gude blue hair,
I wad hae gi'en them off my hurdies,          buttocks
For ae blink o' the bonie burdies!          moment, girls

   But wither'd beldams, auld and droll,
160 Rigwoodie hags wad spean a foal,          withered, wean
Lowping and flinging on a crummock,          jumping, crook
I wonder didna turn thy stomach.

   But *Tam* kend what was what fu' brawlie,          full well
There was ae winsome wench and wawlie,          good-looking
That night enlisted in the core,
(Lang after kend on *Carrick* shore;
For mony a beast to dead she shot,
And perish'd mony a bony boat,
And shook baith meikle corn and bear,          both, barley
170 And kept the country-side in fear:)
Her cutty sark, o' Paisley harn,          short, linen
That while a lassie she had worn,          girl
In longitude tho' sorely scanty,

It was her best, and she was vauntie. —     vain/proud
Ah! little kend thy reverend grannie,
That sark she coft for her wee Nannie,     bought
Wi' twa pund Scots, ('twas a' her riches),     two pounds
Wad ever grac'd a dance of witches!     would have

But here my Muse her wing maun cour;     cower
180   Sic flights are far beyond her pow'r;
To sing how Nannie lap and flang,     leapt, kicked
(A souple jade she was, and strang),     supple wench
And how *Tam* stood, like ane bewitch'd,
And thought his very een enrich'd;     eyes
Even Satan glowr'd, and fidg'd fu' fain,     twitched with excitement
And hotch'd and blew wi' might and main:     fidgeted
Till first ae caper, syne anither,     then
*Tam* tint his reason a' thegither,     lost
And roars out, 'Weel done, Cutty-sark!'
190   And in an instant all was dark:
And scarcely had he Maggie rallied,
When out the hellish legion sallied.

As bees bizz out wi' angry fyke,     buzz, commotion
When plundering herds assail their byke;     hive
As open pussie's mortal foes,
When, pop! she starts before their nose;
As eager runs the market-crowd,
When 'Catch the thief!' resounds aloud;
So Maggie runs, the witches follow,
200   Wi' mony an eldritch skreech and hollow.     unearthly shriek

Ah, *Tam*! Ah, *Tam*! thou'll get thy fairin!     just reward
In hell they'll roast thee like a herrin!
In vain thy *Kate* awaits thy comin!
*Kate* soon will be a woefu' woman!
Now, do thy speedy utmost, Meg,
And win the key-stane[1] of the brig;     bridge

---

[1] It is a well known fact that witches, or any evil spirits, have no power to follow a poor wight any farther than the middle of the next running stream. – It

There at them thou thy tail may toss,
A running stream they dare na cross.
But ere the key-stane she could make,
210  The fient a tail she had to shake!                    Never a
For Nannie, far before the rest,
Hard upon noble Maggie prest,
And flew at *Tam* wi' furious ettle;                     aim
But little wist she Maggie's mettle –
Ae spring brought off her master hale,                   completely
But left behind her ain grey tail:
The carlin caught her by the rump,
And left poor Maggie scarce a stump.

Now, wha this tale o' truth shall read,
220  Ilk man and mother's son, take heed:
Whene'er to drink you are inclin'd,
Or cutty-sarks run in your mind,
Think, ye may buy the joys o'er dear,
Remember Tam o' Shanter's mare.


# To A Haggis


Fair fa' your honest, sonsie face,                       plump
Great Chieftan o' the Puddin-race!                       Pudding
Aboon them a' ye tak your place,                         above
           Painch, tripe, or thairm:                     stomach, intestines
Weel are ye wordy o' a grace                             well worthy
           As lang's my arm.                             long

The groaning trencher there ye fill,
Your hurdies like a distant hill,                        buttocks

may be proper likewise to mention to the benighted traveller, that when he falls in with *bogles*, whatever danger may be in his going forward, there is much more hazard in turning back.

Your *pin* wad help to mend a mill                    skewer
10            In time o' need,
While thro' your pores the dews distil
            Like amber bead.                          drop of whisky


His knife see Rustic-labour dight,                    wipe
An' cut you up wi' ready slight,
Teaching your gushing entrails bright
            Like onie ditch;                          any
And then, O what a glorious sight,
            Warm-reekin, rich!                        -steaming


Then, horn for horn they stretch an' strive, spoon
20 Deil tak the hindmost, on they drive,             devil take the last
Till a' their weel-swall'd kytes belyve              all  well-swollen  bellies,
            Are bent like drums;                      soon
Then auld Guidman, maist like to rive,               master, almost fit burst
            *Bethankit* hums.                         hums the Grace


Is there that owre his French *ragout*,              over
Or *olio* that wad staw a sow,                       oil would satiate
Or *fricassee* wad mak her spew                      make
            Wi' perfect sconner,                      disgust
Looks down wi' sneering, scornfu' view
30            On sic a dinner?                        such


Poor devil! See him owre his trash,
As feckless as a' wither'd rash,                     weak withered rush
His spindle shank a guid whip-lash,                  skinny leg good
            His nieve a nit;                          fist, nut
Thro' bluidy flood or field to dash,
            O how unfit!


But mark the Rustic, *haggis-fed*,
The trembling earth resounds his tread,
Clap in his walie nieve a blade,                     ample fist
40            He'll mak it whissle;                   make whistle
An' legs, an' arms, an' heads will sned,             trim
            Like taps o' thrissle.                    tops, thistle

Ye Pow'rs wha mak mankind your care,
And dish them out their bill o' fare,
Auld Scotland wants nae stinkin ware     watery
          That jaups in luggies;     spills, little bowls with handles
But, if ye wish her gratefu' pray'r,
          Gie her a *haggis!*     give

# Death and Doctor Hornbook. A True Story

Some books are lies frae end to end,
And some great lies were never penn'd;
Ev'n Ministers they hae been kenn'd,     known
          In holy rapture,
Great lies and nonsense baith to vend,     both
          And nail't wi' Scripture.

But this that I am gaun to tell,     going
Which lately on a night befel,
Is just as true's the Deil's in h-ll,
10           Or Dublin city:
That e'er he nearer comes oursel
          'S a muckle pity,     great

The Clachan yill had made me canty,     village ale
I was na fou, but just had plenty;     drunk
I stacher'd whyles, but ye took tent ay     staggered at times, care
          To free the ditches;
An' hillocks, stanes, an' bushes kenn'd ay     always
          Frae ghaists an' witches.     ghosts

The rising moon began to glowr
20 The distant *Cumnock* hills out-owre;     over
To count her horns, wi' a' my pow'r,
          I set mysel;
But whether she had three or four,
          I cou'd na tell.     could not

I was come round about the hill,
And todlin down on *Willie's mill*,    *tottering*
Setting my staff wi' a' my skill,
      To keep me sicker;    *sure*
Tho' leeward whyles, against my will,
30       I took a bicker.    *stagger*

I there wi' *Something* does forgather,
That pat me in an eerie swither;    *put, doubt*
An awfu' scythe, out-owre ae shouther,    *one shoulder*
      Clear-dangling, hang;
A three-tae'd leister on the ither    *toed, trident, other*
      Lay, large an' lang.

Its stature seem'd lang Scotch ells twa,    *roughly a yard long*
The queerest shape that e'er I saw,
For fient a wame it had ava,    *no, stomach, at all*
40       And then its shanks,
They were as thin, as sharp an' sma',
      As cheeks o' branks.    *horse bridles*

'Guid-een' quo' I; 'Friend! Hae ye been    *Good evening*
   mawin,    *mowing*
'When ither folk are busy sawin?'    *sowing*
It seem'd to make a kind o' stan',
      But naething spak;    *said nothing*
At length, says I, 'Friend, whare ye gaun,
      'Will ye go back?'

It spak right howe – 'My name is *Death*,    *hollow*
50 'But be na' fley'd.' – Quoth I, 'Guid faith,    *afraid*
'Ye're maybe come to stap my breath;    *stop*
      'But tent me, billie;    *attend to, my man*
'I red ye weel, tak care o' skaith,    *advise, injury*
      'See, there's a gully!'    *large knife*

'Gudeman,' quo' he, 'put up your whittle,    *knife*
'I'm no design'd to try its mettle;
'But if I did, I wad be kittle    *would be likely*

            'To be mislear'd,            misunderstood
'I wad na' mind it, no that spittle
60              'Out-owre my beard.'

'Weel, weel!' says I, 'a bargain be't;
'Come, gies your hand, an' sae we're gree't;   give, so agreed
'We'll ease our shanks an' tak a seat,
            'Come, gies your news!
'This while ye hae been mony a gate,     have, many
            'At mony a house.'

'Ay, ay!' quo' he, an' shook his head,
'It's e'en a lang, lang time indeed
'Sin' I began to nick the thread,
70             'An choke the breath:
'Folk maun do something for their bread,   must
            'An' sae maun *Death*.

'Sax thousand years are near hand fled    six
'Sin' I was to the butching bred,
'And mony a scheme in vain's been laid,
            'To stap or scar me;
'Till ane Hornbook's tae'n up the trade,
            'And faith, he'll waur me.    worst

'Ye ken *John Hornbook* i' the Clachan,    village
80 'Deil mak his king's-hood in a spleuchan!  entrails, tobacco pouch
'He's grown sae weel acquaint wi' *Buchan*,  medical book
            'And ither chaps    other
'The weans haud out their fingers laughin,  children hold
            'And pouk my hips.   pluck

'See, here's a scythe, and there's a dart,
'They hae pierc'd mony a gallant heart;
'But Doctor *Hornbook*, wi' his art
            'And cursed skill,
'Has made them baith no worth a f–t,
90            'D—n'd hae't they'll kill!

''Twas but yestreen, nae farther gaen,      last night
'I threw a noble throw at ane;
'Wi' less, I'm sure, I've hundreds slain;
      'But deil-ma-care!      devil
'It just play'd dirl on the bane,      knock, bone
      'But did nae mair.

'*Hornbook* was by, wi' ready art,
'And had sae fortify'd the part,
'That when I looked to my dart,
100      'It was sae blunt,
'Fient haet o't wad hae pierc'd the heart      not a bit of it would
      'Of a kail runt.      cabbage stem

'I drew my scythe in sic a fury,      such
'I nearhand cowpit wi' my hurry,      tumbled
'But yet the bauld *Apothecary*      bold
      'Withstood the shock;
'I might as weel hae try'd a quarry
      'O' hard whin-rock.      hard

'E'en them he canna get attended,
110      'Altho' their face he ne'er had kend it,
'Just sh – in a kail-blade and send it,      cabbage leaf
      'As soon's he smells 't.
'Baith their disease, and what will mend it,
      'At once he tells 't.

'And then a' doctor's saws and whittles,
'Of a' dimensions, shapes, an' mettles,
'A' kinds o' boxes, mugs, an' bottles,
      'He's sure to hae;
'Their Latin names as fast he rattles
120      'As A B C.

'Calces o' fossils, earths, and trees;      powders
'True Sal-marinum o' the seas;      sea salt
'The Farina of beans and pease,      vegetable meal
      'He has 't in plenty;
'Aqua-fontis, what you please,      fresh water
      'He can content ye.

'Forbye some new, uncommon weapons,
'Urinus Spiritus of capons;                      urine
'Or Mite-horn shavings, filings, scrapings,
130          'Distill'd *per se*;
'Sal-alkali o' Midge-tail clippings,             salt
          'And mony mae.'                        more

'Waes me for *Johnny Ged's Hole* now'            Alas! The grave digger
Quoth I, 'if that thae news be true!
'His braw calf-ward whare gowans grew,           enclosure for calves,
          'Sae white an' bonie,                  daisies
'Nae doubt they'll rive it wi' the plew;         dig up, plough
          'They'll ruin *Johnie*!'

The creature grain'd an eldritch laugh           groaned, weird
140  And says, 'Ye needna yoke the pleugh.       plough
'Kirk-yards will soon be till'd eneugh,          enough
          Tak ye nae fear:
'They'll a' be trench'd wi' mony a sheugh,       ditch
          'In twa-three year.

'Whare I kill'd ane, a fair strae-death,         death in bed
'By loss o' blood, or want o' breath,
'This night I'm free to tak my aith,             oath
          'That *Hornbook's* skill
'Has clad a score i' their last claith,          cloth, shroud
150          'By drap and pill.                  drop

'An honest Wabster to his trade,                 weaver
'Whase wife's twa nieves were scarce             fists
          weel-bred,
'Gat tippence-worth to mend her head,            twopence
          'When it was sair;
'The wife slade cannie to her bed,               slid, carefully
          'But ne'er spak mair.

'A countra Laird had ta'en the batts             colic
'Or some curmurring in his guts,                 murmuring

‘His only son for *Hornbook* sets,
160          ‘And pays him well,
‘The lad, for twa guid gimmer-pets,          good young pet ewes
          ‘Was Laird himsel.

‘A bonie lass, ye kend her name,
‘Some ill-brewn drink had hov’d her wame,          swelled, belly
‘She trusts hersel, to hide the shame,
          ‘In *Hornbook’s* care;
‘*Horn* sent her aff to her lang hame          off, death
          ‘To hide it there.

‘That’s just a swatch o’ *Hornbook’s* way,
170 ‘Thus goes he on from day to day,
‘Thus does he poison, kill, an’ slay,
          ‘An’s weel pay’d for ’t;          and is well paid
‘Yet stops me o’ my lawfu’ prey
          ‘Wi’ his d–mn’d dirt!

‘But hark! I’ll tell you of a plot,
‘Tho’ dinna ye be speakin o’t;          don’t
‘I’ll nail the self-conceited Sot,
          ‘As dead’s a herrin:
‘Niest time we meet, I’ll wad a groat,          next, bet, threepence
180          ‘He gets his fairin!’          Scots
                    just reward

But just as he began to tell,
The auld kirk-hammer strak the bell          struck
Some wee short hour ayont the *twal*          beyond twelve
          Which rais’d us baith:          made . . . get up
I took the way that pleas’d mysel,
          And sae did *Death*.

# Address to the Unco Guid, or the Rigidly Righteous

## I

O ye wha are sae guid yoursel,                              so, good
    Sae pious and sae holy,
Ye've nought to do but mark and tell
    Your Neebour's fauts and folly!                  neighbour's faults
Whase life is like a weel-gaun mill,                        whose, well-going
    Supply wi' store o' water,
The heapet happer's ebbing still,                           well-filled hopper's
    And still the clap plays clatter.                clapper of the mill

## II

Hear me, ye venerable Core,
10    As counsel for poor mortals;
That frequent pass douce Wisdom's door                      prudent
    For glaikit Folly's portals;                     foolish
I, for their thoughtless, careless sakes,
    Would here propone defences,
Their donsie tricks, their black mistakes,                  hapless
    Their failings and mischances.

## III

Ye see your state wi' theirs compared,
    And shudder at the niffer,                       comparison
But cast a moment's fair regard,
20    What maks the mighty differ;
Discount what scant occasion gave,
    That purity ye pride in,
And (what's aft mair than a' the lave)                      often more, all, rest
    Your better art o' hiding.

## IV

Think, when your castigated pulse
    Gies now and then a wallop,
What ragings must his veins convulse,
    That still eternal gallop:
Wi' wind and tide fair i' your tail,

30          Right on ye scud your sea-way:
        But, in the teeth o' baith to sail,       *both*
           It makes an unco leeway.      *odd*

V

See Social Life and Glee sit down,
        All joyous and unthinking,
Till, quite transmugrify'd, they're grown    *transformed*
        Debauchery and Drinking:
O would they stay to calculate
        Th' eternal consequences:
Or your more dreaded h–ll to state,
40        Damnation of expences!

VI

Ye high, exalted, virtuous Dames,
        Ty'd up in godly laces,
Before ye gie poor *Frailty* names,
        Suppose a change o' cases;
A dear-lov'd lad, convenience snug,
        A treacherous inclination –
But, let me whisper i' your lug,       *ear*
        Ye're aiblins nae temptation.    *perhaps*

VII

Then gently scan your brother Man    *criticize*
50        Still gentler sister woman;
Tho' they may gang a-kennin wrang,    *go a little wrong*
        To step aside is human:
One point must still be greatly dark,
        The moving *Why* they do it;
And just as lamely can ye mark,
        How far perhaps they rue it.

VIII

Who made the heart, 'tis *He* alone
        Decidedly can try us,
He knows each chord its various tone,
60        Each spring its various bias:
Then at the balance let's be mute,

We never can adjust it;
What's *done* we partly may compute,
But know not what's *resisted*.

# Notes

***The Twa Dogs*** Drafted probably by November 1785, completed by mid-February 1786 (Burns to John Richmond, 17 February 1786; Richmond, 1765–1846, was one of Burns's intimates from the Mauchline period, a lawyer's clerk first in Gavin Hamilton's office there and later in Edinburgh). Burns's brother Gilbert explained that the poet's dog Luath, a great favourite, had been 'killed by the wanton cruelty of some person' the night before their father died (13 February 1784). 'Robert said to me, that he should like to confer such immortality as he could bestow upon his old friend *Luath*, and that he had a great mind to introduce something into the book under the title of *Stanzas to the Memory of a quadruped Friend*; but this plan was given up for the tale as it now stands. Caesar was merely the creature of the poet's imagination.'

Burns knew Fergusson's satirical dialogue poem 'Mutual Complaint of Plainstanes and Causey [pavement and street] in their Mother-tongue' (1773), written, like this poem, in octosyllabic couplets. With the example of Fergusson's deftly rendered colloquial Scots speech in mind, he has created a highly original form of social satire, using canine 'characters' to express pointed criticism. Fergusson has no such animal creations as Burns; indeed, only the Fables of the 15th-century poet Robert Henryson offer anything in Lowland Scots comparable to the astonishingly authentic blend of animal and human characteristics found in Caesar and Luath.

Part of the secret of Burns's success lies in the strategic skill with which he shows Caesar, the rich man's Newfoundland, kept as a pet, to be no stand-offish snob with his nose in the air, but on the contrary a willing companion for the 'gash an' faithfu' *tyke*' Luath, ready to share with him dogs' interests – and to talk – on equal terms. Not only is Caesar's freedom from class pretension in itself a means of commenting on the pettiness of human divisions. His genial outlook wins the goodwill of the reader: he is no biased observer of the life of the gentry, but instead a reliable witness, who can be trusted completely. His revelations carry weight therefore, and when he offers his summing-up, the tone of fair and deliberate judgment damns the life-style of the well-to-do much more effectively than a less carefully dramatized argument could possibly do:

> There's some exceptions, man an' woman;
> But this is Gentry's life in common.

**2 coil:** Kyle, Burns's native, middle district of Ayrshire (cf. 'The Vision'). 'King Kyle' was the land within this district between the Ayr and the Doon. **11 some place far abroad:** Newfoundland. 'A large breed of dog, noted for its sagacity, good temper, strength . . .' (*OED*), introduced to Britain in the 18th century. **27 in *Highland sang*:** 'Cuchullin's dog in Ossian's Fingal' (footnote by Burns). Controversy had raged for twenty years over James Macpherson's claim that *Fingal* (1762) was a translation of 'an ancient Epic'. Dr Johnson agreed with David Hume's comment that 'he would not believe the authenticity of *Fingal*, though fifty barearsed highlanders should swear it'. **51 racked rents:** Rents in Ayrshire rose sharply in the agrarian revolution, some landlords exploiting the situation very unfairly. **65 Our Whipper-in:** Hugh Andrew, who served Hugh Montgomerie of Coilsfield, Tarbolton. **96 a *factor's* snash:** 'My father's generous Master died [Provost Fergusson, in 1769]; the farm [Mount Oliphant] proved a ruinous bargain; and, to clench the curse, we fell into the hands of a Factor who sat for the picture I have drawn of one in my Tale of two dogs . . . my indignation yet boils at the recollection of the scoundrel tyrant's insolent, threatening epistles' (Burns to Dr John Moore, 2 August 1787, *Letters* I. 136–7). **119 *patronage an' priests*:** The Patronage Act of 1712 had reasserted the rights of lay patrons (usually local landowners) to appoint ministers to parishes of the Church of Scotland; but many people fiercely resisted this, believing that the right should lie instead with congregations. Another point of contention concerned the theological outlook of ministers, who were sometimes categorized – according to their beliefs – as 'Auld Licht' (strictly orthodox) or 'New Licht' (liberal). **181 breakin o' their timmer:** The common people living on the land were often bitterly opposed to the large-scale tree planting which went on in the second half of the 18th century under the influence of 'improving' lairds. Saplings and young trees planted in country estates were sometimes destroyed under cover of darkness.

***Scotch Drink*** Written between November 1785 and mid-February 1786 (letter to John Richmond, 17 February 1786). On 20 March 1786 Burns wrote to his friend Robert Muir, wine-merchant in Kilmarnock: 'I here inclose my SCOTCH DRINK, and "may the – follow with a blessing for your edification". – I hope, sometime before we have the Gowk [cuckoo], to have the pleasure of seeing you, at Kilm^k; when I intend we shall have a gill between us, in a Mutchkin-stoup; which will be a great comfort and consolation . . .', (*Letters* I. 29). Fergusson's poem 'Caller Water' is Burns's precedent for using the 6-line 'Standart Habby' stanza (see p. 28) in a poem celebrating the rejection of wine for another kind of drink. Compare with the opening of 'Scotch Drink', 'Caller Water', ll. 19–24:

> The fuddlin' Bardies now-a-days
> Rin *maukin*-mad in Bacchus' praise,
> And limp and stoiter thro' their lays
> > *Anacreontic*,
> While each his sea of wine displays
> > As big's the Pontic.

**17 *John Barleycorn*:** The grain from which malt liquor is made. **28 oil'd by thee:** cf. Ramsay, 'Epistle to Robert Yarde', ll. 105–8:

> A cheerfu' Bottle sooths the Mind,
> Gars Carles grow canty, free and kind;
> Defeats our Care, and hales our Strife,
> And brawly oyls the Wheels of Life.

**41 pirratch:** This form has manuscript authority, though Burns changed it to the more usual *parritch* in his 1787 edition. **70 Wae worth . . . Gies famous sport:** Toned down in 1787 to:

> Wae worth the name!
> Nae Howdie [midwife] gets a social night,
> > Or plack [coin] frae them.

**84 spier her price . . . *Brandy*, burnan trash!:** In Fergusson's 'A Drink Eclogue', ll. 63–4, whisky says to brandy:

> For now our Gentles gabbs are brown sae nice,
> At thee they toot, an' never speer my price.

**109 Thee *Ferintosh*! O sadly lost!:** Whisky distilled at Ferintosh on the Cromarty Firth had been exempt from duty since 1695 in reparation for damage (caused in 1689 by the Jacobites) to the estates of Forbes of Culloden, who owned the distillery. In 1785 the exemption was withdrawn. Although more than £20,000 was paid in compensation, the price of whisky rose. Burns's poem reflects the continuing keen interest in the subject in Scotland from the consumer's viewpoint. **115 curst horse-leeches o' th'Excise:** Ironical, considering that Burns was later to accept employment himself as an exciseman.

***The Holy Fair*** 'Composed in 1785' (note by Burns on the Kilmarnock MS), probably after the Mauchline annual Communion, held on the second Sunday in August. Mauchline had only 400 communicant church members, but it is known that in 1786 no fewer than 1,400 received the sacrament, and there is no reason to think such a number was unusual. A

Holy Fair went on the several days before reaching its climax in the Communion service; people came from far and wide to hear the 'preachings'. Hence the pretext for communal involvement on the scale and of the boisterous sort described by Burns. In real life, as in Burns's poem, noisy rival factions supported 'Auld Licht' (evangelical) and 'New Licht' (moderate) preachers; hard drinking went on in Nanse Tinnock's tavern next to the churchyard; and many country-dwellers got into the habit of treating the series of religious meetings as a prelude to letting their hair down.

Burns's first aim is to amuse by creating a lively and convivial scene. His companion Fun, however, directs laughter specifically at Superstition and Hypocrisy (stanzas III to V). 'The Holy Fair' quickly becomes a social satire which turns on a series of contrasts between lofty pretensions and lowly performance, between loudly professed religious motives and actual human inclinations – which prove too strong to resist – to booze, quarrel, and fornicate.

Behind the poem lies a long tradition of Scottish vernacular verse, from the medieval 'brawl' poems 'Chrystis Kirk of the Grene' and 'Peblis to the Play' to Robert Fergusson's 'Leith Races' and 'Hallow-Fair'. Burns borrows his metrical form from Fergusson, and broadly keeps to the traditional combination of playful irony and vigorous social description. Certain details point to his also having read *A Letter from a Blacksmith to the Ministers and Elders of the Church of Scotland* (1759). However, 'The Holy Fair' displays a highly original thematic unity. Burns gives depth and meaning to the vividly rendered particulars which belong to his satirical celebration. His early 19th-century biographer J. G. Lockhart noted accurately that, with the publication of this poem, 'national manners were once more in the hands of a national poet'.

**Title:** 'Holy Fair is a common phrase in the West of Scotland for a sacramental occasion' (Burns, in his 1787 edition). **Epigraph:** From a satire by Tom Brown directed against Jeremy Collier, *The Stage Beaux toss'd in a Blanket; or, Hypocrisie Alamode* (1704). **5 GALSTON:** A village a few miles north of Mossgiel. **37 My name is FUN:** cf. Fergusson's account in 'Leith Races' of his meeting with Mirth, a 'laughing lass', whom he takes as his companion for the day (*Poems*, STS, ii. 160–1). **41–5 to \*\*\*\*\*\*\*\*\* holy fair:** cf. 'Leith Races', ll. 37–45:

> A bargain be't, and, by my feggs,
> > Gif ye will be my mate,
> Wi' you I'll screw the cheery pegs,
> > Ye shanna find me blate;
> We'll reel an' ramble thro' the sands,
> > And jeer wi' a' we meet . . .

cf. also Burns's 'Epistle to J. L*****k', ll. 103–6. **61 *sweet-milk cheese*:** A special treat. 'The milk, the cheese, the butter were reserved by the thrifty housewife from the family with jealous care, that they might be converted into cash' (John Mitchell, DD, *Memories of Ayrshire about 1780*, ed. W. K. Dickson, Scottish History Society, Miscellany, vi. 1939, (p. 272). **66 *black-bonnet*:** The officiating elder wore a black cap of traditional design. **75 *racer* Jess:** Janet Gibson, the half-witted daughter of 'Poosie Nansie' (Agnes Gibson), who kept a disreputable tavern in the Cowgate, Mauchline. Jess ran errands for her mother. **86 an *Elect* swatch:** Amended in 1787 to 'a Chosen swatch'. **91 O happy is that man, an' blest!:** Burns here quotes line 1 of verse 2 from the Scottish metrical version of Psalm 146, which may be being sung even as the scene he describes is enacted. **102 ****** speels the holy door:** Identified as 'Sawnie' in two manuscripts. Alexander Moodie (1728–99), minister of Riccarton from 1762, said once to have preached to his congregation on John 8:44, 'Ye are of your father the devil, and the lusts of your father ye will do.' **103 tidings o' s-lv-t-n:** Changed in 1787 to 'tidings o' d-mn-t-n' after Dr Hugh Blair, minister of the High Kirk in Edinburgh and Professor of Rhetoric in Edinburgh University, had objected that the original 'gives just offence. The Author may easily contrive some other Rhyme in place of the word Salv—n.' **104 *Hornie*, as in ancient days:** cf. Job 1:6, 'Now there was a day when the sons of God came to present themselves before the Lord, and Satan came also among them.' **116 *cantharidian* plaisters:** Plasters of cantharides (Spanish fly), an aphrodisiac. **122 ***** opens out his cauld harangues:** MS 'Geordie begins his . . .' George Smith (d. 1823), a 'New Licht' moderate, minister of Galston. The preaching of such ministers was dismissed by the 'Auld Licht' evangelicals as insipid, mere morals without faith. Here, Smith's sermon sends off the godly in search of drink. **131 ANTONINE:** Roman emperor and reformer. **138 *******, frae the water-fit:** MS 'Willy'. Rev. William Peebles (1753–1826), of Newton-upon-Ayr, clerk of the Ayr Presbytery. Burns describes him in 'The Holy Tulzie' as 'shaul' (shallow). Peebles never forgave Burns, and in 1811 published verses scorning 'Burnomania', the rise of the Burns cult. **142 COMMON-SENSE:** Traditionally identified as the poet's friend Dr John Mackenzie of Mauchline. **145 Wee ****** niest:** MS 'M—R'. Alexander Miller, 'the assistant minister at St Michael's (Burns, in a copy of the Kilmarnock edition); from 1788 minister of Kilmaurs, where his presentation by the Earl of Eglinton led to violent opposition from the congregation. Miller was short and very stout. **184 Black ******:** John Russel (*c.* 1740–1817), previously schoolmaster at Cromarty, ordained as minister at Kilmarnock in 1774; notorious for his severity of temper and doctrine. **188 'Sauls does harrow'**: *Hamlet* I, v, 15ff., 'I could a Tale unfold . . . harrow up thy soul.' **226 *Clinkumbell*:** The town-crier, bellman. **231 lasses strip their shoon . . .** : Burns's way of ending 'The Holy Fair' shows that he has borrowed hints from Ramsay's addition to 'Chrystis Kirk of the Grene' (Ramsay, *Works*, STS, i, 73):

> And unko Wark that fell at E'en,
> Whan Lasses were haff winkin,
> They lost their Feet and baith their Een,
> And Maidenheads gae'd linkin
> Aff a' that Day.

**237 hearts o' stane:** Burns plays boldly on Ezekiel 36:26: 'A new heart also will I give you, and a new spirit will I put within you: and I will take away the stony heart out of your flesh, and I will give you an heart of flesh.'

*Address to the Deil* Written in the winter of 1785–6: Burns refers to it as completed in his letter to Richmond of 17 February 1786. While he has no exact model for a comic invocation of this degree of boldness, vernacular Scots tradition is rich in reductive humour concerning the supernatural – born in part out of fear. This humour is made the basis of this art in 'Address to the Deil'. Burns clearly enjoys taking a radically different attitude to his subject from Milton in *Paradise Lost*. The poem begins as an exercise in the medieval craft of 'flyting' or scolding in verse; but as it develops, it anticipates 'Halloween' and 'Tam o' Shanter' as an ironic portrayal of still powerful, though waning, popular beliefs. Burns calls the Devil by a series of familiar, disrespectful nicknames (Hornie, Nick, Clootie, Hangie), bringing him down to his own level and robbing him of dignity. He then goes on to enumerate traditional beliefs, concerning the actions of the Devil and of his agents on earth, warlocks and witches, before gently dismissing Satan as an enemy whose measure he has taken.

The poem was more sexually explicit in manuscript, and also more personal, than appears from the printed version. Lines 61–6 originally contained a bawdy joke about a bridgroom interrupted in his love-making by evil spells:

> Thence, knots are coosten, spells contriv'd,
> An' the brisk bridegroom, newly wived
> Just at the kittle point arriv'd,
> Fond, keen, an' croose,
> Is by some spitfu' jad depriv'd
> O's warklum's use.

When Burns was revising his *Poems* for the 1787 Edinburgh edition, the critic Hugh Blair suggested that the (toned down) stanza printed in 1786 'had better be left out, as indecent': Burns did not act on this advice. A different motive had in 1786 led the poet to replace manuscript ll. 89–90 containing a direct tribute to Jean Armour:

> Langsyne, in Eden's happy scene,
> When strappin Edie's days were green,
> An' Eve was like my bonie Jean,
> My dearest part,
> A dancin, sweet, young, handsome quean
> Wi' guileless heart.

This change seems to have been made shortly before publication – by the summer of 1786 Burns was estranged from Jean. With regard to the stanza immediately following, there was certainly no love lost between Burns and Jean's father; and Burns may also have thought of 'Daddie' Auld, a minister friendly to the Armours, in the role of killjoy 'snick-drawing dog' driving Jean and himself out of Paradise.

**Epigraph:** *Paradise Lost*, i, 128–9. cf. letter to William Nicol of 18 June 1787, 'I have bought a pocket Milton, which I carry perpetually about with me, in order to study the sentiments – the dauntless magnanimity; the intrepid unyielding independance; the desperate daring, and noble defiance of hardship, in that great Personage, Satan.' (*Letters* I. 123). **1 O Thou:** An echo of Pope's way of addressing Swift in *The Dunciad*, i, 19–20:

> O Thou! whatever title please thine ear,
> Dean, Drapier, Bickerstaff, or Gulliver!

**2 Auld Hornie:** Traditional Scottish nickname for the horned Devil. 'Nick' may be a form of Nicholas (reason obscure), while 'Clootie' means 'cloven-hoofed'. **19 roaran lion:** I Peter 5:8, 'your adversary the devil, as a roaring lion, walketh about, seeking whom he may devour'. **21 strong-wing'd Tempest:** Tradition had it that the Devil raised strong winds. **35 boortries:** Elder trees were supposed to give protection against witchcraft. **45 stoor:** 'sounding hollow, strong, and hoarse' (B). **50 ragweed:** Witches were said to ride on many kinds of steed – animals, enchanted humans, ragwort, ash branches, or straws. **61 mystic knots:** Knots devised in malice by witches. **63 *wark-lume*:** According to a 17th-century tract, *Satan's Invisible World Discovered*, witches sometimes meddled with the weaver's craft. Burns uses the word with a sexual meaning. **69 *Water-kelpies*:** Water-demons in the shape of horses, bent on drowning travellers (traditional in the Scottish Highlands). Burns wrote to Cunningham on 10 September 1792 of 'a Kelpie, haunting the ford, or ferry, in the starless night, mixing thy laughing yell with the howling of the storm' (*Letters* II. 145). **73 *Spunkies*:** ('As for Willy and the Wisp, he is a fiery devil, and leads people off their road in order to drown them, for he sparks sometimes at our feet, and then turns before us with his candle, as if he were twa or three miles before us, many a good boat has Spunkie drown'd' (Dougal Graham, *History of Buckhaven in Fifeshire*, 1806). **79 When MASONS' mystic *word* an' *grip*:** Burns refers to the Masonic password and handshake as having force to stir up the Devil in a storm; then by contrast to the tradition that a cock, cat, or other unchristened creature was needed in order to appease the Devil. A joke at the expense of Masons, including the poet himself. **85 Lang syne in EDEN's bonie yard:** cf. Fergusson, 'Caller Water', ll. 1–2 (*Poems*, STS, ii, 106):

> When father Adie first pat spade in
> The bonny yeard of antient Eden.

By July 1786 Burns was estranged from Jean Armour, and this stanza replaces one in the Kilmarnock MS (see introductory note, above).
**91 snick-drawing:** '*An auld sneck-drawer*, one who, from long experience, has acquired a great degree of facility in accomplishing any artful purpose' (*Jamieson's Scots Dictionary*). **107 lows'd his ill-tongu'd, wicked *Scawl*:** cf. Job 2:8–10, 'Thou speakest as one of the foolish women speaketh.' **111 MICHAEL:** cf. *Paradise Lost*, vi. 320, 'then Satan first knew pain . . .'. **123–4 Ye aiblins might . . . hae a *stake*:** cf. Sterne, *Tristram Shandy*, III, xi: 'I declare, quoth my uncle Toby, my heart would not let me curse the devil himself . . . But he is cursed and damned already, to all eternity, replied Dr Slop. I am sorry for it, quoth my uncle Toby.'

*The Death and Dying Words of Poor Mailie* Burns's first sustained poem in Scots, included in his First Commonplace Book in an entry dated June 1785, but written considerably earlier. According to his brother Gilbert, he had 'partly by way of frolic, bought a ewe and two lambs from a neighbour, and she was tethered in a field adjoining the house at Lochlea. He and I were going out with our teams, and our two younger brothers to drive for us, at mid-day, when Hugh Wilson, a curious-looking, awkward boy, clad in plaiding, came to us with much anxiety in his face, with the information that the ewe had entangled herself in the tether, and was lying in the ditch. Robert was much tickled with Huoc's appearance and postures on the occasion. Poor Mailie was set to rights, and when we returned from the plough in the evening he repeated to me her *Death and Dying Words* pretty much in the way they now stand.'

**Poor Mailie's Elegy** Written to accompany 'The Death and Dying Words of Poor Mailie', but possibly not until Burns had decided to publish his poems. Here he follows a very distinctive tradition of comic elegy in Scots, making use of the 6-line stanza employed by Robert Sempill of Beltrees in *The Life and Death of Habbie Simpson* in the late 17th century, and more recently by William Hamilton of Gilbertfield in his *Last Words of Bonny Heck, a Famous Greyhound*. Allan Ramsay, who named the verse form 'Standart Habby' after the first example above, had used it for familiar epistles, as well as for elegy. Fergusson continued this tradition; and Burns in turn widened the range of the stanza still further, handling it so often and with such success that it came to be known after his death as 'the Burns stanza'. See, for example, 'To J. S****' and 'The Vision'.

**To J. S****** The first of seven verse-epistles included in *Poems, Chiefly in the Scottish Dialect*. Written when Burns had already decided to publish his poems, in the winter of 1785–6 . . .

> This while my notion's taen a sklent,
> To try my fate in guid, black *prent*. (ll. 37–8)

James Smith, six years younger than Burns, was the son of a merchant in Mauchline, and at this time was himself a draper there. Along with John Richmond and the poet, he was one of the self-styled 'Court of Equity', a 'ram-stam' (l. 165) bachelor trio who met in the Whitefoord Arms Inn in Mauchline. Burns celebrated their rakish activities in a riotous mock-trial poem, 'The Court of Equity', which was not published in his lifetime. Smith proved a staunch friend to Burns during his troubles with Jean Armour's family. He worked for a time as a calico-printer in Linlithgow, subsequently emigrating to Jamaica, where he died young.

The poem follows the pattern established in Scots verse-epistles by Ramsay and Fergusson. Beginning with greetings and compliments to Smith, Burns moves on to discuss questions of mutual interest, before returning to a brief final salutation. A particularly lively passage explains Burns's reasons for rhyming (ll. 19–30). His colloquial Scots modulates into lightly accented English in the reflective central part of the poem (ll. 55–120); then he slips back into the vernacular.

**14 scrimpet stature:** This stanza, with its jest about Smith's diminutive stature, was a late addition to the poem in manuscript. **25 Some rhyme . . . :** This much-quoted stanza replaced an earlier manuscript version:

> Some rhyme because they like to clash,
> An' gie a neebor's name a lash;

> An' some (vain thought) for needfu' cash;
>> An' some for fame;
> For me, I string my dogg'rel trash
>> For fun at hame.

**133 DEMPSTER:** George Dempster (1732–1818), Whig MP and agricultural improver.

***The Auld Farmer's New-Year-Morning Salutation to His Auld Mare, Maggie*** In the Kilmarnock MS, this poem followed 'Address to the Deil', which is mentioned in a letter of 17 February 1786; the likeliest date of composition, therefore, is early 1786. Burns glosses 'The Auld Farmer's Salutation' with particular care in the Kilmarnock edition, noting the precise meaning of words as used by farmers in Ayrshire. His aim in the poem, written in the 'Standart Habby' stanza, is to convey the nature of the long and close relationship between farmer and favourite mare. He does this with realism, humour and tenderness. Avoiding excessive sentimentality, he suggests that they have grown old together naturally and with grace. The poem is addressed to Maggie throughout, but – with characteristic country humour – there is a hint that the farmer has affectionately identified together in his mind since his wedding-day (l. 32) Maggie the wedding-gift with his bride Jenny. Jenny has no doubt had to work just as hard as the loyal mare which once belonged to her father.

**Title:** A 'hansel' is a gift to mark a new beginning or special occasion, particularly a New Year gift. **21 o' tocher clear:** Clear of, i.e. quite apart from dowry. **35 KYLE-STEWART:** the northern part of Kyle, Burns's district of Ayrshire, between the rivers Ayr and Irvine. **37 hoyte:** 'the motion between a trot and gallop' (B). **51 *Brooses*:** races at country-weddings, between the bridegroom's home and the bride's home or church. **57 *Scotch mile*:** longer than the standard English mile by some 200 metres. **61 *Fittie-lan'*:** The 'fit-o'-land' or left horse of the back pair in the plough team of four, which trod unploughed land while its partner walked in the furrow. **71 Till sprittie knows . . . :** Until rushy hillocks would have roared and torn away easily. An example of apt rural Scots which may have given difficulty even in 1786. **79 *car*:** A kind of 'sledge', without wheels, made of two long birch or hazel branches, with wicker cross-pieces. The front ends were tied as shafts to the horse's collar while the rear ends were on the ground. **100 fow:** A firlot, equivalent to almost one bushel of wheat or two bushels of barley and oats. Also used in the sense of a 'mow', that which has been forked. **106 To some hain'd rig . . . :** The last three lines replace the MS reading:

An' clap thy back,
An' mind the days we've haen the gither,
An' ca' the crack.

***The Cotter's Saturday Night*** Written in the winter of 1785–6 – the
setting is November (l. 10) – and mentioned by Burns as complete in his
letters to Richmond of 17 February 1786. The father of the household in the
poem is modelled at least in part on Burns's own father, William Burns, who
had died in 1784, worn out by toil on poor land. His piety and concern for
his children's education led him to compile *A Manual of Religious Belief in a
Dialogue between Father and Son*. Burns's brother Gilbert, who shared the
same upbringing as the poet, comments on the central action in the poem,
'Robert had frequently remarked to me that he thought that there was
something peculiarly venerable in the phrase, "Let us worship God", used
by a decent sober head of a family introducing family worship [l. 108]. To
this sentiment . . . the world is indebted for "The Cotter's Saturday Night".'

Burns had a model for a naturalistic word-picture of a domestic farm
scene in Fergusson's 'The Farmer's Ingle', written like his own poem in
Spenserian stanzas. In a number of ways, however, 'The Cotter's Saturday
Night' differs sharply from Fergusson's poem. Whereas 'The Farmer's Ingle'
is wholly in Lowland Scots, Burns combines the vernacular with extended
passages in English. This is because he is concerned to show the nature of
the religious outlook and moral values of those he describes, while
Fergusson's aim is genre description *per se*. The accepted language for
religious and moral reflection in poety in 18th-century Lowland Scotland
was not Scots but English, which had been used in Bible and worship since
the time of the Scottish Reformation. Again in contrast to Fergusson, who
does not identify any love-interest among the members of his farming
family, Burns with the story of Jenny and her wooer introduces a narrative
episode centring on romantic love. This helps to broaden his poem's appeal.
He has been heavily criticized by a number of 20th-century critics for the
rather strained note he strikes in stanza x ('Is there, in human form, that
bears a heart – . . .'). But the communicative power of the whole poem is not
in doubt. In its ambitious scope and tonal range 'The Cotter's Saturday
Night' goes beyond Fergusson's reach in 'The Farmer's Ingle'.

**Dedication:** R. A\*\*\*\*: Robert Aiken (1739–1807), solicitor and surveyor
of taxes in Ayr, eldest son of an Ayr shipbuilder, and grandson of James
Dalrymple, sheriff-clerk of Ayrshire. He met Burns *c.* 1783, and became a
trusted friend and enthusiastic admirer of Burns's poems. He was a talented

public speaker and reader of poetry; Burns commented that 'he read me into fame'. Aiken collected the names of 145 subscribers for the Kilmarnock edition. **10 November chill:** Burns owes something to the opening of Fergusson's poem 'The Farmer's Ingle':

> Whan gloming grey out o'er the welkin keeks,
>> Whan *Batie* ca's his owsen to the byre,
> Whan *Thrasher John*, sair dung, his barn-door steeks,
>> And lusty lasses at the dighting tire . . .

but he also has in mind Gray's *Elegy*, ll. 2–3:

>> The lowing herd wind slowly o'er the lea,
>> The ploughman homeward plods his weary way.

**13 black'ning trains:** Thomson describes 'a blackening train of clamorous rooks' in 'Winter', ll. 140–1. **21ff. The expectant *wee-things*:** Burns's original Scots rendering of a domestic scene which recurs in 18th-century poetry, with its ultimate source in Virgil's *Georgics*, Book II. cf. Gray's *Elegy*, ll. 21–4. **22 flichterin:** Glossed by Burns in 1787 as 'to flutter as young nestlings when their dam approaches'. **23 His wee-bit ingle:** cf. Ramsay, *The Gentle Shepherd*, I, ii, 179–80:

>> In Winter, when he toils thro' Wind and Rain,
>> A blazing Ingle, and a clean Hearth-stane.

**26 *kiaugh* and care:** Revised in 1793 to 'carking cares', possibly because 'kiaugh' seemed obscure. **48 wi' an eydent hand:** cf. 'The Farmer's Ingle', l. 29, 'to labouring lend an evidant hand'. **50 'fear the LORD alway!':** Burns recalls such texts as Psalm 34:9. **73 O happy love!:** Burns writes in his First Commonplace Book, April 1783: 'If anything on earth deserves the name of rapture or transport it is the feelings of green eighteen in the company of the mistress of his heart when she repays him with an equal return of affection.' **82ff. Is there, in human form . . . :** A modern critic has described this stanza as 'one of the most nauseating ever published by a reputable poet' (T. Crawford, *Burns: A Study of the Poems and Songs*, 1960, p. 179); but the poet's moral reflections held strong appeal for his contemporaries. James Kinsley accurately comments that the passage is 'an eighteenth-century set piece' (*The Poems and Songs of Robert Burns*, Oxford, 1968, p. 1115). **93 *Hawkie*:** Cow with the white face, pet name. **96 weel-hain'd kebbuck:** 'If cheese was to be kept for some time . . . all the whey had to be squeezed out, and pressing was a necessity . . . Ayrshire or Dunlop cheese became the country's national cheese.' (A. Fenton, *Scottish Country Life*, 1976, pp. 152, 154.) **111–13 *Dundee . . . Martyrs . . . Elgin*:** Old psalm tunes, the first two being included in the Twelve 'Common Tunes' in the Scottish Psalter of 1615, and 'Elgin' in the Scottish Psalter of 1625.

**115 *Italian trills* are tame:** Burns agrees with Fergusson ('Elegy on the Death of Scots Music', ll. 49–54) in deploring the fashionable preference for elaborate Italian musical performance over native Scottish 'simplicity'; cf. also William Hamilton of Bangour, who describes in Ode IV (*Poems on Several Occasions*, 1760) how cottagers

> Had, at the sober-tasted meal,
> Repeated oft, the grateful tale;
> Had hymn'd, in native language free,
> The song of thanks to heaven and thee;
> A music that the great ne'er hear,
> Yet sweeter to th'internal ear,
> Than any soft seducing note
> E'er thrill'd from Farinelli's throat.

**117 Nae unison hae they:** the Scottish tradition in psalmody was for everyone to keep the same pitch and sing together, in unison. **119 How Abram:** cf. Genesis 12:1–2. **120–1 Moses . . . Amalek:** cf. Exodus 17:9, 16. **122 the *royal Bard* did groaning lye:** cf. Samuel 12:10–11, and Psalm 6. **130 Had not . . . whereon to lay His head:** cf. Matthew 8:20, Luke 9:58. **131–2 How . . . to many a land:** Burns recalls Acts and the New Testament epistles. **133 *he*, who lone in *Patmos*:** cf. Revelation 1:8, 19:17. **135 Bab'lon's doom:** cf. Revelation 18:10. **138 'springs exulting':** *Windsor Forest* ll. 111–12. **141 No more . . . the bitter tear:** cf. Isiah 25:8; Revelation 7:17. **142 hymning their CREATOR's praise:** cf. *Paradise Lost*, vii. 258–9: '. . . hymning prais'd God and his Works, Creatour him they sung'. **153 *Book of Life*:** cf. Revelation 3:5, 13:8. **158 HE who stills the *raven's* clam'rous nest:** cf. Job 38:41, 'Who provideth for the raven his food? when his young ones cry unto God . . .' **159 And decks the lily fair:** cf. Matthew 6:28, 'Consider the lilies of the field . . .' **163 From scenes like these:** Burns echoes Thomson, 'Summer', ll. 423–4:

> A simple scene! yet hence Britannia sees
> Her solid grandeur rise.

**165 Princes and lords:** cf. Goldsmith, *The Deserted Village*, ll. 53–5:

> Princes and lords may flourish, or may fade;
> A breath can make them, as a breath has made:
> But a bold peasantry . . .

**166 'An honest man . . .':** An echo of Pope, *Essay on Man*, iv. 248. **168 The *Cottage* leaves the *Palace*:** Perhaps suggested by Fergusson's Retirement', ll. 45–7:

> In yonder lowly cot delight to dwell,
> And leave the statesman for the labouring hind,

> The regal palace for the lowly cell.

**172 O SCOTIA!:** Fergusson had written in 'The Farmer's Ingle', ll. 113–17:

> May SCOTIA's simmers ay look gay and green,
>> Her yellow har'sts frae scowry blasts decreed;
> May a' her tenants sit fu' snug and bien,
>> Frae the hard grip of ails and poortith freed,
>> And a lang lasting train o' peaceful hours succeed.

**181 the *patriotic tide*:** William Wallace, victor of Stirling Bridge, was executed by Edward I of England in 1305. 'The story of Wallace poured a Scottish prejudice in my veins which will boil along there till the flood-gates of life shut in eternal rest' (*Letters* I. 136). **188 the *Patriot*, and the *Patriot-Bard*:** cf. Coila's speech to the poet in 'The Vision', ll. 109ff.

*To a Mouse* Dated by the poet November 1785. Burns's brother Gilbert stated that the 'verses to the *Mouse* and *Mountain-daisy*' were composed . . . 'while the author was holding the plough'. John Blane, who worked with Burns as gaudsman (driving the horses in front of the plough), commented many years after the event that he, being only a lad, had actually started to run after the mouse with the intention of killing it, when he was checked by Burns; the latter then became 'thoughtful and abstracted'. Whatever the degree of accuracy of Blane's recollection, 'To a Mouse' conveys very directly Burns's tender concern for a defenceless creature. Drawing aptly and unobtrusively on the Bible, and also on the poet's reading of Johnson's *Rasselas*, it wryly underlines two ideas – the unity of creation, and the vulnerability of human beings as well as of small animals.

**6 pattle:** A small long-handed spade carried on a plough to clear it of mud, a plough-staff. **7–8 Man's dominion . . . Nature's social union:** The idea of man as tyrant over the rest of creation is common in 18th-century poetry. cf. Pope, *Essay on Man*, iii. 147–64, and Thomson's *Seasons*, *passim*, e.g. 'Spring', ll. 702–5. **15 *daimen-icker*:** Ayrshire Scots, denoting an occasional ear of corn. Thrave: two stooks of corn, or 24 sheaves, a measure of straw or fodder. **17 I'll get a blessin wi' the the lave:** cf. 'When thou cuttest down thine harvest in thy field, and hast forgot a sheaf in the field, thou shalt not go again to fetch it: it shall be for the stranger, for the fatherless, and for the widow: that the Lord thy God may bless thee in all the work of thine hands' (Deuteronomy 24:19). **22 foggage:** 'rank grass which has not been eaten in summer, or which grows among grain, and is fed on by horses and cattle after the crop is removed' (*Jamieson's Scots Dictionary*). **43–8 Still, thou art blest, compar'd wi' me!:** cf. Johnson, *Rasselas*, chapter 2, 'As he passed through the fields, and saw the animals around him, "Ye," said he, "are happy, and need not envy me that walk thus among you, burdened with myself; nor do I, ye gentle beings, envy your felicity, for it is not the felicity of man. I have many distresses from which ye are free; I fear pain when I do not feel it; I sometimes shrink at evils recollected, and sometimes start at evils anticipated: surely the equity of Providence has balanced peculiar sufferings with peculiar enjoyments.'

*To a Mountain-Daisy* Written in April 1786, during Burns's trouble with Jean Armour's family. He wrote to John Kennedy from Mossgiel on 20 April, '. . . I have here, likewise, inclosed a small piece, the very latest of my productions. I am a good deal pleas'd with some sentiments myself, as they are just the native querulous feelings of a heart, which, as the elegantly melting Gray says, "Melancholy has marked for her own".' (Kennedy, 1757–1812, was factor to the Earl of Dumfries, and later to the Earl of Breadalbane; he received copies of several of Burns's poems in manuscript and was active in securing subscriptions for the Kilmarnock edition.) 'To a Mountain-Daisy' won the praise of early reviewers, Henry Mackenzie drawing attention to it as an example of 'the tender and the moral'. Recent critics, however, have tended to prefer 'To a Mouse' – on which, to some degree, the later poem is modelled – as being stronger in diction and less strained in sentiment than 'To a Mountain-Daisy'.

*Epistle to a Young Friend* Dated in the MS at Kilmarnock 15 May 1786. The 'young friend' of the title was Ayr lawyer Robert Aiken's son Andrew, subsequently a merchant in Liverpool and British consul in Riga. (After Burns's death, William Niven of Kirkoswald claimed that the poem was originally addressed to him. He had, however, kept no copy to make good his case.)

The double stanza, with feminine rhyme, was familiar to Burns from the example of Ramsay.

In preparing the poem for publication, Burns reversed the order of stanzas III and IV, and omitted a MS stanza after VI:

> If ye hae made a step aside,
>      Some hap-mistake, o'ertaen you;
> Yet, still keep up a decent pride,
>      An' ne'er owre far demean you.
> Time comes wi' kind, oblivious shade,
>      An' daily darker sets it;
> An', if nae mae mistakes are made,
>      The world soon forgets it.

**15 views:** Plans, purposes. **87–8 may ye better reck the *rede*:** cf. *Hamlet*, I, iii. 47–51:

> Doe not as some ungracious Pastors doe,
> Shew me the steepe and thorny way to Heaven;
> Whilst like a puft and recklesse Libertine
> Himselfe, the Primrose path of dalliance treads,
> And reaks not his own reade.

***On a Scotch Bard Gone to the West Indies*** Written when Burns had decided to emigrate. His earliest reference to the idea is in a letter of *c.* 20 April 1786 to John Arnot: 'Already the holy beagles, the houghmagandie pack [fornication pack, i.e. the Kirk Session], begin to snuff the scent, & I expect every moment to see them cast off, & hear them after me in full cry [because of Jean Armour's pregnancy]: but as I am an old fox, I shall give them dodging and doubling for it; & by & bye, I intend to earth among the mountains of Jamaica' (*Letters* I. 37). The position Burns had in view was that of book-keeper on a plantation at Port Antonio. By the time of publication of his *Poems*, he had 'orders within three weeks at farthest to repair aboard the Nancy, Cap^n Smith, from Clyde, to Jamaica, and to call at Antigua' (to John Richmond, 30 July 1786). The date of sailing was put off from week to week, however, and by early October 'the feelings of a father' prevented Burns from emigrating (letter to Robert Aiken, *c.* 8 October). He did not entirely give up the idea then, writing to James Smith as late as June 1787 'if I do not fix, I will go for Jamaica'.

Turning on a theme which to most people would not immediately suggest humour, 'On a Scotch Bard Gone to the West Indies' is nevertheless a defiantly playful poem, a fluent and full-blooded exercise in Scots comic elegy. On the stanza, see introductory note on 'Poor Mailie's Elegy', p. 92. **20ff Hadst thou taen aff some drowsy bummle:** Burns boasts about his own sexual prowess ('gleg as onie wumble'), contrasted with 'some drowsy' bungler. **25 KYLE may weepers wear:** Burns's native district of Ayrshire. 'Weepers' were thin stripes of linen worn on the cuffs to denote mourning. **33 A Jillet:** Jean Armour. **56 Your native soil was right ill-willie:** Burns has in mind his own Ayrshire parish, and long experience of uneconomic farms.

***To a Louse*** Probably written in late 1785. That year saw several balloon flights over Scotland by the Italian Vincenzo Lunardi, who gave his name to a balloon-shaped bonnet (l. 35): the gently satirical poem is up-to-date in its reference to fashion. In 18th-century Scotland the louse was a common sight. Burns enjoys the idea that this particular louse evidently does not know its place; it is no respecter of Jenny's airs and graces. The success of the poem comes from Burns's mastery of the 'Standart Habby' verse form. He creates, and manages to sustain, a familiar conversational tone, almost a church whisper, by turns 'shocked' and amused, to match the cheeky movement of the louse on the unsuspecting girl's showy bonnet; and incidentally comments on the congregation's response to Jenny:

> Thae *winks* and *finger-ends*, I dread,
>
> Are notice takin!

Burns's intimate way of speaking to the louse, as to a naughty child, is reminiscent of the technique used in 'Address to the Deil'.

***Epistle to J. L\*\*\*\*\*k*** John Lapraik (1727–1807) was a tenant farmer who had fallen on hard times: in 1785 he was imprisoned for debt in Ayr. While in prison, he wrote poetry for diversion. Following Burns's example, he published *Poems on Several Occasions* at Kilmarnock in 1788. His last years were spent as postmaster and innkeeper in Muirkirk.

Burns's first epistle to Lapraik shows him taking the initiative in contacting a stranger, a fellow-poet of the district, and defining his own characteristic priorities as a writer. The opening describes a 'rocking', a particular kind of social evening when songs and stories were to the fore. Burns responds to the personal (husband to wife) motif in the song by Laspraik which he hears sung. (Years later, he was to send a version of Lapraik's song to James Johnson for inclusion in *The Scots Musical Museum*.) He then goes on to project an image of himself as a spontaneous and instinctive 'rhymer', with no need for academic or critical pretensions ('Gie me ae spark o' Nature's fire . . .', ll. 73–8). His hope is to catch a spark of the inspiration which burns in Allan Ramsay and Fergusson. Reaffirming his wish to meet Lapraik as a friend and 'hae a swap o' *rhyming-ware*', he strongly rejects by contrast the values of people whose efforts are directed towards money-making.

**7 a rockin:** The Rev. John Sheppard of Muirkirk described a rocking as taking place 'when neighbours visit one another in pairs, or three or more in company, during the moonlight of winter or spring . . . The custom seems to have arisen when spinning on the *rock or distaff* was in use, which therefore was carried along with the visitant to a neighbour's house, [and] still prevails, though the *rock* is laid aside' (*Memories of Ayrshire about 1780*, ed. W. Kirk Dickson, Scottish History Society, Miscellany vi, 1939, p. 288).
**13 *ae sang*:** 'When I upon thy bosom lean', said to have been written when Lapraik's wife had been fretting over their misfortunes. Lapraik included the

song in his *Poems on Several Occasions* (Kilmarnock, 1788), and Burns supplied an improved version in Scots for *The Scots Musical Museum* (no. 205, 1780). **21–2 Pope ... Steele ... Beattie**: Here as examples of writers skilled in expressing moral sentiments. Burns was familiar with the poetry of Pope, and with Steele's periodical essays. James Beattie (1735–1803), professor of moral philosophy at Aberdeen, was best known for his blank-verse poem, *The Minstrel*, although he also wrote Scots verse. **24 About *Muirkirk*:** Lapraik lived at Dalfram, on Ayr Water, about nine miles from Mauchline, and near the village of Muirkirk. **28–30 The version of these lines in the First Commonplace Book reads:**

> He was a devil
> But had a frank & friendly heart
> Discreet & civil.

**45 *crambo-jingle*:** cf. Hamilton of Gilbertfield, Epistle I to Allan Ramsay, ll. 49–50.

> At Crambo then we'll rack our Brain,
> Drown ilk dull Care and aiking Pain.

**61f What's a' your jargon:** cf. Pomfret, *Reason* (1700), ll. 57–8:

> What's all the noisy jargon of the schools
> But idle nonsense of laborious fools ...

**73 Gie me ae Spark:** cf. Sterne, *Tristram Shandy*, III, xii, 'Great Apollo! if thou art in a giving humour – give me – I ask no more, but one stroke of native humour, with a single spark of thy own fire along with it.' **79 ALLAN:** Allan Ramsay. **80 FERGUSSON:** Robert Fergusson. 'Rhyme, except some religious pieces, which are in print, I had given up; but meeting with Fergusson's Scotch Poems, I strung anew my wildly-sounding, rustic lyre with emulating vigour' (letter to John Moore, August 1787). **103 MAUCHLINE Race or MAUCHLINE Fair:** In suggesting a convivial meeting between poets, Burns follows the example of Hamilton of Gilbertfield in his first Epistle to Ramsay. Hamilton writes, 'At Edinburgh we'll hae a Bottle of reaming claret' (l. 45).

*Song, It was upon a Lammas night* Burns stated that this song was written before his twenty-third year: the actual time of composition is unrecorded. He was to note many years after 1786, 'All the old words that ever I could meet to this [air] were the following, which seem to have been an old chorus:–

> O corn rigs and rye rigs,
>   O corn rigs are bonie,
> And when'er you meet a bonnie lass,
>   Preen up her cockernony.'

He also knew Ramsay's song 'My Patie Is a Lover Gay' from *The Gentle Shepherd*, which ends

> Then I'll comply and marry Pate,
> And syne my Cockernonny
> He's free to touzel air or late
> Where Corn-rigs are bonny.

In performance, this is one of Burns's most successful love-songs, proving that he was able even at this early date to match his words to the spirit of a traditional tune. In comparison with Ramsay's song, 'It was upon a Lammas night' is thoroughly personal. Whereas Ramsay offers a conventional example of pastoral verse love-description, tinged with genteel eroticism, Burns writes in the first person and achieves a note of delight in remembered passion. The identity of Annie is not known, although the youngest daughter of John Rankine (see previous poem and introductory note) later claimed the honour. The tune probably originated in Scotland, although its 17th-century printings are English.

**1 Lammas:** 1 August, harvest festival when new bread was consecrated. Here the sense is 'late summer', or more specifically 'harvest night in August'. **2 rigs:** Broad arable ridges which sloped towards ditches. **5 head:** Burns changed this word to 'heed' in the 1793 edition. The phrase 'tentless heed' occurs to 'To J. S****', l. 55.

*Song 'Now westlin winds'* Written in 1775 at the time of Burns's infatuation with Peggy Thomson of Kirkoswald. 'I spent my seventeenth summer,' he wrote in his autobiographical letter to Dr Moore in August 1787, 'on a smuggling [coast] a good distance from home at a noted school, to learn Mensuration, Surveying, Dialling, &c . . . I went on with a high hand in my Geometry; till the sun entered Virgo, a month which is always a carnival in my bosom, a charming Fillette who lived next door to the school overset my Trigonomertry, and set me off in a tangent from the sphere of my studies.' Later, he tried out a modification of this early song in honour of Jean Armour; no known copy survives. Going back to the same song, Burns then sent a version which has a number of Scots words in place of the original English diction to be printed in *The Scots Musical Museum* (vol. iv, 1792, no. 351). Unusually for a love-song, 'Now westlin winds' includes four lines of protest against the 'slaught'ring guns' of sportsmen (ll. 21–4).

*A Bard's Epitaph* Possibly written not long after the 'Epistle to a Young

Friend', which is dated 15 May 1786. Burns describes himself as a man 'whose judgment clear, /Can others teach the course to steer' (ll. 13–14).

He wrote several poems in a wry confessional vein, showing self-knowledge and also the ability to laugh at himself. A well-known example is the 'Elegy on the Death of Robert Ruisseaux', with its revealing final stanza:

> Tho' he was bred to kintra wark,
> And counted was baith wight and stark,
> Yet that was never Robin's mark,
>     To mak a man;
> But tell him, he was learn'd and dark,
>     Ye roos'd him then!

Though sombre in comparison, 'A Bard's Epitaph' is in its own way no less characteristic, recalling in its concluding lines the practical advice offered in the 'Epistle to a Young Friend'.

***Holy Willie's Prayer*** Burns wrote 'Holy Willie's Prayer' early in 1785, after the Presbytery of Ayr ordered the erasure of a Mauchline Kirk Session minute which alleged neglect of public worship by the poet's friend and landlord Gavin Hamilton. One of the charges against Hamilton was that he caused his servant to pick potatoes on the Sabbath – hence Willie's curse in l. 78. William Fisher (1737–1809), a Mauchline elder since 1772, was a leading figure in the case against Hamilton, as Burns's prose headnote to the poem shows. Burns also refers to the Rev. William Auld (1709–91), minister of Mauchline since 1742, and to Robert Aiken (cf. note on 'The Cotter's Saturday Night'). After giving rise to considerable local ill will, the case ended in July 1787 when the Session of Mauchline granted Hamilton a certificate freeing him from ecclesiastical censure; but as Burns explained to Dr Moore,

> [the poem] alarmed the kirk-Session so much that they held three separate meetings to look over their holy artillery, if any of it was pointed against profane Rhymers. Unluckily for me, my idle wandering led me, on another side [i.e. illicit sex], point-blank within reach of their heaviest metal . . . (*Letters*, letter 125, l. 144)

Willie's prayer follows the traditional pattern of invocation and praise (ll. 1–30); confession and penitence (ll. 37–60); intercession and petition (ll. 61–102). Burns's satirical aim is to let Willie Fisher's words reveal hypocrisy and worldliness – this would-be paragon of the virtues of the Elect is completely unaware that his own words prove him to be a fraud and drunken lecher. The satire is thus sharply personal, but Burns uses the particular instance to convey rejection of doctrinaire Calvinism and a general attack on constricting religious attitudes.

**3 Sends ane to heaven and ten to h-ll:** The Calvinist doctrine of double predestination. Cf. the Westminster Confession (1643), iii: 'Neither are any redeemed by Christ . . . but the elect only. The rest of mankind God was pleased . . . to pass by.' **13 generation:** family, line. **17 Sax thousand years:** The traditional dating of the Creation, 4004 BC, in the 710th year of the Julian period. **18 Thro' Adam's cause:** Romans 5. 12–19, 'by one man sin entered into the world, and death by sin'. **27 a pillar o' thy temple:** Revelation 3. 12, 'Him that overcometh will I make a pillar in the temple of my God.' **35 For I am keeper by thy fear:** In October 1790, Fisher was solemnly rebuked by Rev. Auld for drunkenness, and warned, 'Be on your guard in all time coming against this bewitching sin, shun bad company, avoid taverns as much as possible, and abhor the character of a tippler' (Chambers-Wallace, i. 190). **55 this fleshly thorn:** cf. Corinthians 12. 7–9, 'lest I should be exalted above measure . . . there was given to me a thorn in the flesh . . . most gladly therefore will I rather glory in my infirmities'. **61 L—d bless thy Chosen:** Burns wrote in 1788 that he was 'in perpetual warfare with that doctrine of our Reverend Priesthood, that "we are born into this world bond slaves of iniquity and heirs of perdition, wholly inclined" to that which is evil . . . untill by a kind of Spiritual Filtration or rectifying process Called effectual Calling &c. – The whole business is reversed . . . We come into this world with a heart and disposition to do good for it, untill by . . . Selfishness, the too precious Metal of the Soul is brought down to the blackguard Sterling of ordinary currency' (letter 261, *Letters*, I. 303).

**Tam o' Shanter** Burns wrote 'Tam o' Shanter', his 'standard performance in the poetical line', in November 1790, sending the completed poem on 1 December to his friend Francis Grose, who had encouraged him to treat in verse the story it contains. Grose (1731–91) was an artist and antiquary, whom Burns met in 1789 when Grose was staying close to him in Nithsdale, collecting materials for *The Antiquities of Scotland*. The two men took to each other instinctively, Burns commenting to Mrs Dunlop, 'I have never seen a man of more original observation, anecdote and remark' (letter 352, *Letters* I. 423). Burns asked Grose to include a drawing of Alloway Kirk in Ayrshire, as it was the burial-place of his father, and offered in return to supply information for the book. A letter to Grose of summer 1790 recounts 'three of the many Witch stories I have heard relating to Alloway Kirk'. The first and second of these provide part of the essential narrative outline and detail which would be used in 'Tam o' Shanter', (ii), being virtually a prose draft of the poem:

(i) Upon a stormy night, amid whirling squalls of wind and bitter blasts of hail, . . . on such a night as the devil would chuse to take the air in, a farmer or farmer's servant was plodding and plashing homeward . . . His way lay by the Kirk of Aloway, and being rather on the anxious look-out in approaching a place so well known to be a favourite haunt of the devil and the devil's friends and emissaries, he was struck aghast by discovering . . . a light . . . proceed[ing] from the haunted edifice. Whether he had been fortified from above on his devout supplication . . . or . . . he had got courageously drunk . . . so it was that he ventured . . . into the very kirk . . . The members of the infernal junto were all out on some midnight business or other, and he saw nothing but a kind of kettle . . . over the fire . . . simmering some heads of unchristened children, limbs of executed malefactors, &c. for the business of the night . . .

(ii) On market day in the town of Ayr, a farmer from Carrick . . . whose way lay by the very gate of Aloway kirk-yard, in order to cross the river Doon at the old bridge . . . had been detained by his business till by the time he reached Alloway it was the wizard hour, between night and morning.

Though he was terrified, with a blaze streaming from the kirk, yet as it is a well-known fact, that to turn back on these occasions is running by far the greatest risk of mischief, he prudently advanced on his road . . . He was surprised and entertained . . . to see a dance of witches merrily footing it round their old sooty blackguard master, who was keeping them all alive with the power of his bagpipe. The farmer stopping his horse to observe them a little, could plainly descry the faces of many old women of his acquaintance and neighbourhood. How the gentleman was dressed, tradition does not say; but the ladies were all in their smocks; and one of them happening unluckily to have a smock which was considerably too short to answer all the purpose of that piece of dress, our farmer was so tickled that he involuntarily burst out, with a loud laugh, 'Weel luppen, Maggy wi' the short sark!', and recollecting himself, instantly spurred his horse to the top of his speed. I need not mention the universally known fact, that no diabolical power can pursue you beyond the middle of a running stream . . . Against he reached the middle of the arch of the bridge . . . the pursuing, vengeful hags were so close at his heels, that one of them actually sprung to seize him; but it was too late, nothing was on her side of the stream but the horse's tail, which immediately gave way to her infernal grip . . . but the farmer was beyond her reach. – However, the unsightly, tail-less condition of the vigorous steed was . . . an awful warning to the Carrick farmers, not to stay too late in Ayr markets (letter 401, *Letters* II. 29–31).

**Epigraph:** From Gavin Douglas, *Eneados*, vi, Prologue, l. 18. The Prologues were included in *Select Works of Gavin Douglas* (Perth, 1787). **13 *Tam o' Shanter*:** Local tradition held that the hero of the poem was suggested by Dougal Graham (1739–1811), tenant of the farm of Shanter on the Carrick shore. He was addicted to convivial evenings in Ayr, and was subject to scoldings from his superstitious wife. Burns knew *John Cheap The Chapman*, a popular chapbook by Dougal Graham which describes the exploits of its chapman hero John and his companion Drouthy Tom. **28 Kirkton Jean:** Traditionally Jean Kennedy, who with her sister Ann kept 'a reputable public-house' in *Kirkoswald*. **32 *Alloway's* auld haunted kirk:** The church gradually fell into disrepair after the parish of Alloway was combined with Ayr in 1690. **41 Souter *Johnny*:** Traditionally John Davidson (1728–1806), who lived near Shanter and was later a cobbler in Kirkoswald, or John Lachlan (d. 1819), shoemaker in Ayr. **116f *Nae cotillion*:** Burns expresses a traditional 18th-century preference for Scots dances. **154 seventeen hunder linnen:** 1,700 threads went into weaving the warp. **160 spean a foal:** frighten it off the teat. **171 Paisley harn:** fine, costly linen.

***To A Haggis*** creates good-humoured verse about a traditional kind of Scottish food. The word probably comes from the Scots verb *hag*, to chop or hack. The recipe for haggis includes the large stomach bag of a sheep and beef, suet, oatmeal, onions, pepper and salt. Burns's poem makes proud but also playful claims for strengths Scots derive from haggis. 'To A Haggis' is recited at Burns Suppers held on or close to 25 January.

***Death and Doctor Hornbook*** is on one level a personal lampoon or satire on the character of a Mauchline schoolmaster John Wilson or 'Jock Hornbook' who also gave medical advice and dispensed drugs – hence the 'Doctor' in the title. A hornbook was a first book for children learning to read, including the alphabet mounted protected by a sheet of transparent horn. The poem mocks at the idea of Death by robbing it of terror and solemnity.

***Address To The Unco Guid*** rejects the narrowness of 'the very good', fault-finders who take it on themselves to criticise the rest of humanity. Burns's sympathies are with the strengths and weaknesses of ordinary people. He suggests

'Then gently scan your brother man,
Still gentler sister woman.'

## Everyman's Poetry

Titles available in this series  **all at £1.00**

**William Blake**
ed. Peter Butter
0 460 87800 X

**Robert Burns**
ed. Donald Low
0 460 87814 X

**Samuel Taylor Coleridge**
ed. John Beer
0 460 87826 3

**Thomas Gray**
ed. Robert Mack
0 460 87805 0

**Ivor Gurney**
ed. George Walter
0 460 87797 6

**George Herbert**
ed. D. J. Enright
0 460 87795 X

**Robert Herrick**
ed. Douglas Brooks-Davies
0 460 87799 2

**John Keats**
ed. Nicholas Roe
0 460 87808 5

**Henry Wadsworth
Longfellow**
ed. Anthony Thwaite
0 460 87821 2

**John Milton**
ed. Gordon Campbell
0 460 87813 1

**Edgar Allan Poe**
ed. Richard Gray
0 460 87804 2

**Poetry Please!**
Foreword by Charles
Causley
0 460 87824 7

**Alexander Pope**
ed. Douglas Brooks-Davies
0 460 87798 4

**Lord Rochester**
ed. Paddy Lyons
0 460 87819 0

**Christina Rossetti**
ed. Jan Marsh
0 460 87820 4

**William Shakespeare**
ed. Martin Dodsworth
0 460 87815 8

**Alfred, Lord Tennyson**
ed. Michael Baron
0 460 87802 6

**R. S. Thomas**
ed. Anthony Thwaite
0 460 87811 5

**Walt Whitman**
ed. Ellman Crasnow
0 460 87825 5

**Oscar Wilde**
ed. Robert Mighall
0 460 87803 4